D0257703

NOTES

Introduction

"I would not have believed that I would ever again be completely enthralled by a story of young children – especially a young girl narrator – growing up in a typical southern town," wrote Katherine Gauss Jackson in *Harper's Magazine* when *To Kill a Mockingbird* came out in 1960. "After all, we had *Member of the Wedding* not so long ago, with... the Negro cook in the kitchen so earthily wise in answering difficult questions when parents are not at hand. And here it all is again, but different."

This one was different all right. For one thing, as part of her growing up this little girl, Scout Finch, had to watch her father Atticus confront their community's racism. Within two years *To Kill a Mockingbird* had been translated into ten languages, won the Pulitzer Prize, emerged as an Oscar-winning film and spent 88 weeks on the American bestseller lists. By 1964 it had sold five million copies; now the book's world sales total over six times that. It has never been out of print, in either hardback or paperback. British librarians have voted it the book they would most recommend. In 1991 a Library of Congress survey of reading habits found that it was one of three books "most often cited as making a difference", second only to the Bible.

Early reviewers welcomed it tepidly, giving no signs of the sensation to come. "Harper Lee's *To Kill a Mockingbird*... is sugar water served with humor," said the august *Atlantic Monthly*. It is "pleasant, undemanding reading". In its "Briefly Noted" section *The New Yorker* provided a notice of just 76 words, 26 of which read: "Miss Lee is a skilled, unpretentious and totally ingenuous writer who slides unconcernedly and irresistibly back and forth between being sentimental, tough, melodramatic, acute, and funny."

While escaping early critical challenge, the novel quickly attracted opposition of another kind. Like *The Catcher in the Rye* (1951), that other 60-million bestseller about childhood, *Mockingbird* was widely banned from local libraries and school curricula from the 1960s through to the 1980s. Those charged with the care of the youth were hypersensitive about what the fictional young should be made to see and hear in novels: words like "damn", "piss", "whore lady" – and (as with *Huckleberry Finn*) "nigger" – even though in the context of a critique of racial prejudice. But the objections went beyond words alone. The story of children being confronted by a rape case seemed inappropriate in a book to be read by real-life children. So did the book's portrayal of "institutionalized racism", as one group of protestors in Indiana put it, "under the guise of 'good literature'".

Set in the author's own youth, when the Great Depression was more on people's minds than the need for racial equality, *Mockingbird* emerged into the ferment of the Civil Rights movement. How well would Atticus Finch's liberal understanding of his neighbours' fear and hatred of "the Negro" – his teaching that in time tolerance of the other would sort the problem out – measure up to the radical activism of James Baldwin and Eldridge Cleaver, or the mass rallies organized by Ralph Abernathy and Martin Luther King to change the law and get it applied?

Another early reviewer called *To Kill a Mockingbird* "a wholesome book on an unwholesome theme". That wholesomeness is partly to do with childhood, the point of view from which the narrator tells her story, but Atticus's authoritative voice conditions the mood too. His critique of white prejudice is gradualist rather than genuinely progressive; it imagines change as coming about first through a transformation in human sympathy before it can be enshrined in the law.

After the turmoil of the Civil Rights movement, after the Vietnam War, after the election of America's first black president, has *To Kill a Mockingbird* come to look like "a period piece", as Harold Bloom has called it? Or does the novel survive, perhaps even transcend historical change? Certainly its popularity remains undimmed, and no one now thinks it unfit for children.

A summary of the plot

The story is told by the tomboy Jean Louise "Scout" Finch, six years old at the start of her narrative. Scout lives with her older brother Jem and their widowed father, the lawyer Atticus Finch, in a "tired old town" in southern Alabama. Their black housekeeper Calpurnia acts as surrogate mother for the children. Jem and Scout play with Dill Harris, who comes to stay with his aunt every summer.

The children are fascinated by their neighbour Arthur "Boo" Radley, who lives unseen with his father in a shuttered old house surrounded by live oaks. The children dare each other to approach the house. Using a fishing pole, Jem tries unsuccessfully to leave a note at Boo's window. One moonlit night they crawl under a barbed wire fence, through the Radleys' field of collard greens, in order to get a glimpse of Boo through his window. A shadow moves across the porch, someone shoots a shotgun in the air, the children scatter, and Jem tears his breeches on the wire, slipping out of them to escape. When he summons up courage to go back for them, he finds his trousers folded up over the fence, the rip sewn up.

On their way to and from school the children often find little gifts in a knothole in one of the big oaks outside the Radley house – trinkets like two Indian-head pennies, a ball of twine and two figurines carved out of soap.

Atticus is charged by the town judge to defend Tom Robinson, an African American accused of raping a white girl. He agrees reluctantly. Townspeople call him "nigger-lover", puzzling and upsetting the children. On the eve of the trial a posse of country people arrives to lynch the defendant. Atticus sits in the jailhouse door reading a newspaper to bar their way. The children arrive to see what's going on, refusing to leave when Atticus orders them to. Scout talks to one of the men, the father of a school friend, asking how he is and sending his boy her greetings. Embarrassed, the men leave the scene.

Next day the children, whom Atticus has forbidden from the trial, hide in the African-American gallery overlooking the courtroom. The prosecution opens the trial by interviewing Tom Ewell, father of the alleged victim, Mayella. He describes hearing her scream, running to the window and looking in to see "that black nigger yonder ruttin' on my Mayella". She had been beaten too, according to the Sheriff, who found her "bunged up" on the right side of her face, with "a black eye comin'" and bruises on her neck and right arm.

Through his adroit questioning of Mayella, her father, and the defendant, Atticus shows that Tom Robinson, whose left arm is paralysed, could never have committed the assault, but that instead

Mayella had propositioned him, been caught in the act and beaten by her father. Atticus's powerful concluding speech for the defence invokes the Declaration of Independence that all men are created equal – if not in everyday life then at least in court. Despite the evidence and Atticus's plea, the jury convicts by a unanimous vote.

Bob Ewell, humiliated by the revelations in court, spits tobacco juice in Atticus's face as he is coming out of the post office. Though Atticus plans to appeal the verdict, Tom Robinson panics and tries to escape from the town jail. He is shot dead while trying to climb the outer fence.

Coming home from a school pageant, Scout and Jem are attacked in the dark. In the struggle Jem's arm is broken, and only Scout's costume saves her from a knife wound. A mysterious stranger interrupts the assault, carrying Jem home while Scout follows. This turns out to be Boo Radley, the source of all those little gifts in the tree, and the children's hidden protector all along.

The town sheriff arrives to reveal that the assailant had been Bob Ewell, and that he has been stabbed – "Fell on his own knife," he insists against Atticus's protest that the law should be allowed to take its course. Scout agrees with the sheriff; otherwise, she says, "It'd be sort of like shootin' a mockingbird, wouldn't it?"

What is *To Kill a Mockingbird* about?

On one level *To Kill a Mockingbird* is about racial prejudice in the southern states of America. The climax of the plot, Tom Robinson's trial and its aftermath, certainly reinforces this theme. And the novel's appearance in the midst of the great civil rights campaign made that story reverberate for contemporary readers.

Early critics certainly experienced *To Kill a Mockingbird* as a shape-changing novel about race. "In the twentieth century," wrote Joseph Crespino, "*To Kill a Mockingbird* is probably the most widely read book dealing with race in America, and its protagonist, Atticus Finch, the most enduring image of fictional heroism." For James Carville, reading the book was like St Paul's conversion on the road to Damascus. As a schoolboy during the Civil Rights turmoil he remembered wishing "the blacks just didn't push so damn hard to change" segregation. Then the woman who drove the mobile library round his neighbourhood suggested he read *To Kill a Mockingbird*.

> I couldn't put it down. I stuck it inside another book and read it under my desk during school. When I got to the last page, I closed it and said, "They're right and we're wrong." The issue was

literally black and white, and we were positively on the wrong side.

Some support to the racial theme, not noticed by the critics, is the fact that almost every white character is slightly odd, and their relationships to others skewed. Scout is a tomboy (about which more later); Dill is "a curiosity": childlike, looking far younger than his age, with snow-white hair, and light blue shorts that button to his shirt instead of the overalls worn by the other children. Boo Radley, whose arrested development has kept him secluded at home for 20 years, is the strangest of all.

Not only that, but there is hardly a conventional marriage or family in the book. Scout's and Jem's mother has died; they are looked after by their black housekeeper, Calpurnia, and see their father Atticus only when he gets home late from work. We don't read of any family weekends spent together, let alone outings or holidays. Aunt Alexandra is married, but estranged from her husband. Across the street lives Miss Maudie, a spinster. Mrs Dubose, an ill and embittered widow addicted to morphine, is two doors down. Dill is only available to play with Scout and Jem because he has been offloaded by his parents, who live separately from each other pursuing their own affairs. Then there's Tom Ewell, who beats his daughter and (it is hinted) sexually abuses her.

In fact the only "normal" nuclear family in the book, though it is only sketched in, not explored imaginatively, is Tom Robinson's, at least until it is torn apart by his false accusation, trial and death.

Does this mean that the white townspeople are socially dysfunctional, while their despised black neighbours are comparatively well adjusted? Possibly, but all talk of themes becomes complicated by Scout's first-person point of view. Everything is seen through her eyes, and although her language is sometimes that of the mature woman writing her, what the reader learns is restricted by the fact that Scout can't be everywhere at once, and that she has the limited understanding of a child, albeit a precocious and likeable one. Scout sees, discovers and thinks so

THE TITLE

The Northern Mockingbird (*Mimus polyglottos*), found in the southern states of America, is a thrush-like bird with a long tail, creamy grey breast and white flashes mid-wing. It is happy to nest near houses, and likes to perch on the lower branches of maple and sycamore trees. It is very vocal and, as its name suggests, can mimic other birds, animals and even mechanical noises like car alarms. It is popular in American folklore, as in the song "Listen to the Mockingbird", and is the official state bird of many things during the course of *To Kill a Mockingbird* that it's difficult for a reader to take away a single theme from the book.

And there are so many other strands in the story beyond race and the trial of Tom Robinson. Boo Radley is clearly a crucial element. Boo stalks the narrative: at first a terror to the children, then in turn a mystery, a secret sharer, a hidden protector, finally their saviour. Scout's changing relationships with her older brother, with Dill, with Calpurnia – above all with her father Atticus – form an important part of the story. So do her reactions to Aunt Alexandra and her missionary circle. Then there is the substantial subplot of the children and Mrs Dubose, when, after a particularly foul outburst from the old lady, Jem

---

Arkansas, Florida, Mississippi, Tennessee and Texas.

The bird functions as the governing metaphor of *To Kill a Mockingbird*, linking the innocence of Tom Robinson and Boo Radley with the natural world around Maycomb. Atticus tells Scout and Jem that he would rather they shot their air rifles at tin cans than birds, but in any case remember that "it's a sin to kill a mockingbird". Scout has never heard Atticus describe anything as a sin; so she asks Maudie for an explanation. "Your father's right," says Maudie. "Mockingbirds don't do one thing but make music for us to enjoy. They don't eat up people's gardens, don't nest in corncribs, they don't do one thing but sing their hearts out for us. That's why it's a sin to kill a mockingbird" (10) ∎

cuts off the heads of all her camellias, then is forced to read Walter Scott to her every afternoon after school for a month.

Having everything filtered through Scout's consciousness makes us aware not only of what has happened but also of how we come to know it. The same goes for the values and judgments that the narrative assigns to people and events. These are Scout's in the first instance. And this is where her own oddness comes in. As something of a loner, she is distant from the town's social conventions, and also indifferent to its moral pieties.

This emotional distance on top of her natural childish naivety make Scout something of a satirist, an amusing observer of everything from her teacher Miss Caroline's "new way they're teaching the first grade", the Dewey Decimal System (really a way of classifying books in a library), to the members of Aunt Alexandra's missionary circle, those "ladies in bunches [who] always fill [Scout] with vague apprehension", wearing their cool "pastel prints", most of them "heavily powdered but unrouged".

But when she expresses an opinion within the action – say, to Jem or Dill, Calpurnia or Atticus – rather than silently to the reader, her point of view is often challenged, if not corrected. When she ridicules Walter Cunningham for pouring syrup all over his meat and vegetables, a furious Calpurnia takes her into the kitchen and rebukes her for her bad manners: "anybody sets foot in this house's yo' company, and don't you let me catch you remarkin' on their ways like you was so high and mighty!" (3). Stung by the taunts of Mrs Dubose, Scout asks her father: "You aren't really a nigger-lover, then, are you?" Atticus answers: "I certainly am. I do my best to love everybody" (11). After Ewell spits on Atticus, threatening future revenge, Atticus advises them to "stand in Bob Ewell's shoes for a minute. I destroyed his last shred of credibility at the trial... The man had to have some kind of comeback" (23).

In other words, Scout is not just a narrative device providing a commentary on the action. She is also a character in the novel – its protagonist in fact – one who develops and grows. By the time of the trial, her charitable sensitivity has even developed to the point where she can feel spontaneous sympathy for Mayella Ewell's loneliness. At the novel's end, thinking back over the years and seasons of their fragmentary encounters with Boo Radley, Scout acknowledges that "Atticus was right... that you never really know a man until you stand in his shoes and walk around in them."

The meaning of *To Kill a Mockingbird*, then, cannot be summed up in a single phrase or slogan. It is explored through a process, traced through a girl's maturing through feeling, of becoming human through the development and exercise of her sympathetic imagination. Beyond that essential education, as Scout muses while walking home from having escorted Boo back to his house, "there wasn't much else left for us to learn, except possibly algebra".

How strong is the influence of real events on the novel?

As a novel with a race-related capital trial at the centre of its plot, *To Kill A Mockingbird* needs to be set in context . The first thing to note is that it relates to two time frames: that of its setting and that of its composition and publication. Set in the Great Depression, the narrative runs from 1933, when Scout is "almost six", to 1935, when she nearly loses her life. Eric Sundquist has pointed out that the rape case of Tom Robinson in 1935 "is set in a small town Alabama courtroom that would inevitably have been reverberating with the impact of the ongoing trials of the Scottsboro Boys... [which] put the South under sensationally national scrutiny".

In the Scottsboro trials nine black teenagers, the youngest of whom were 12 and 13, were sentenced to death for allegedly raping two white girls. The trials and retrials lasted an astonishing six years, from 1931 to 1937. They were indeed a national sensation, leading to two successful

The Scottsboro Boys in jail, 1931

appeals to the U. S. Supreme Court, not to mention
the more general popular outrage generated by
coverage in the press outside the South.

What happened was this. On March 25, 1931,
the nine boys were riding the rails – hitching an
illicit lift on a freight train – between Chattanooga
and Memphis, Tennessee, in search of jobs. Four
young white men and two women were also on the
train. Not long after the line dips down into the

northeast corner of Alabama the black and white boys got into a fight, with the result that the white boys were forced off. Bent on revenge, they reported the fight to the stationmaster at Stevenson, Alabama, who telegraphed ahead to Paint Rock to have the train stopped and the blacks arrested.

It was at this point that the two white women accused the blacks of raping them. The boys were immediately taken to jail in nearby Scottsboro. A lynch mob gathering outside the jail later in the same day was dispersed when the state governor called out the National Guard.

The first of many trials of the Scottsboro Boys was scheduled for April 6, 1931, just twelve days after their arrest. For the defence the state appointed an elderly local lawyer who hadn't tried a case in decades and an unpaid real estate agent, acting as *amicus curiae*, or friend of the court. They had no time to prepare a defence, even if they had known how to. Victoria Price, one of the alleged victims of the rape, testified for the prosecution at great length, but was cross-examined for only ten minutes. The only witnesses for the defence were the defendants themselves, who were confused and offered conflicting testimony. The defence offered no closing statement. To no one's surprise the accused were convicted of rape and sentenced to death. At this point the American Communist Party stepped in and got the verdicts appealed to the State Supreme Court, which upheld all but one of the convictions and sentences. Meanwhile, the case went all the way to the U. S. Supreme Court, who ruled, in the landmark case of *Powell v. Alabama* (1932), that the incompetence of the defence had denied the defendants the citizen's right to due process of law, and that the case would have to be retried.

The retrials began on March 30, 1933. Now the state stepped up its game, appointing the Alabama Attorney General, Thomas Knight Jr, as chief prosecutor. Not to be outfaced, the Communist International Labor Defense (ILD) persuaded a high-powered attorney, Samuel Leibowitz, to act for the Scottsboro Boys, *pro bono*. Leibowitz, funded by "Jew money from New York" – as assistant prosecutor Wade Wright would put it – was no Communist, but a staunch Democrat. This time the defence paid serious attention to the medical evidence. Dr R. R. Bridges, who had examined the alleged victims two hours after the alleged rapes, testified that he had found no lacerations or vaginal tears to suggest rape, and that the sperm in Price's vagina was nonmotile. Together these findings suggested she had had consensual intercourse at least 24 hours before the rape was supposed to have taken place.

The defence's cross-examination of Victoria Price was merciless. Leibowitz was able to show that almost every detail of her former testimony was false. He then produced a surprise witness. This was none other than Ruby Bates, the other alleged victim, who had moved to New York after the first trial. Bates testified that she and Price were prostitutes, that no rape had taken place, and that when the two women were picked up in Alabama, Price advised her to "frame up a story" as a smokescreen to prevent their own arrest for violating the Mann Act forbidding the crossing of state lines "for immoral purposes".

With the prosecution's case suddenly deflated, the presiding judge, James E. Horton, had no choice but to set aside the verdict and sentences. He was an honest man, described by reporters from the northern papers as looking like Abraham Lincoln without the beard. He was also brave, because he was a circuit judge, up for re-election in the following year, a contest which he duly lost. The utter discrediting of Victoria Price's testimony should have put the state on its guard, but not a bit of it. It took four more years of trials of the various defendants and yet another appeal to the U. S. Supreme Court before in 1937 Alabama finally dropped charges against four of the accused. The others would avoid the death penalty and eventually escape or jump parole.

Apart from the reverberations of the Scottsboro trials, no very great effort is made to locate *To Kill a Mockingbird* within its historical time frame, the

Great Depression and the New Deal. There are occasional references in the novel to hard times (especially on farms), relief checks and New Deal agencies like the Works Progress Administration (WPA), but nothing to convince the reader that the history of the 1930s is an integral part of the plot.

In fact, the reference to the WPA in Chapter Two, where Atticus explains to Scout that Mr Cunningham cannot take a WPA job because it would mean neglecting his farm, is anachronistic. Scout is "almost six" at this point in the novel, and Jem "nearly ten", which makes the year 1933. The WPA was not set up until 1935.

Similarly, when in the meeting of Aunt Alexandra's missionary circle in Chapter 24 Mrs Merriweather objects to Eleanor Roosevelt "coming down to Birmingham and tryin' to sit with 'em", the year is 1935, whereas the First Lady did not take her seat with the black delegates to the Southern Conference on Human Welfare in Birmingham, Alabama, until 1938.

Patrick Chura, who notes these anachronisms, thinks the contexts contemporary with the composition of *To Kill a Mockingbird* are much more important than the historical ones. "Because the text's 1930s history is superficial," he writes, "the novel is best understood as an amalgam or cross-historical montage, its 'historical present' diluted by the influence of events and ideology concurrent with its period of production."

Without doubt, the overriding contemporary context was the great movement for African-American civil rights, already under way as Harper Lee was writing the novel and continuing after it was published. The Civil Rights movement started with *Brown v. Board of Education* (1954) – or more precisely, with the South's reaction to that crucial Supreme Court judgment, and other people's response to that reaction.

In *Brown v. Board of Education of Topeka* (to give the decision its full name) the Supreme Court overturned the old Court decision of *Plessy v.*

HARPER LEE AND TRUMAN CAPOTE

Born in New Orleans in 1924, Truman Capote was sent to live with a distant relative in Lee's home town of Monroeville, Alabama, after his parents divorced. "Mr and Mrs Lee, Harper Lee's mother and father... lived very near," he later recalled. "Harper Lee was my best friend. Did you ever read her book, *To Kill a Mockingbird*? I'm a character in that book, which takes place in the same small town in Alabama where we lived."

As different as they were in personality, Lee and Capote shared a love of writing and a determination to succeed. He too used Monroeville as the setting of his first novel, *Other Voices, Other Rooms* (1948), now best remembered for Harold Halma's epicene photograph of the author on the back of the dust

Ferguson (1896), which held that state laws mandating racial segregation were constitutional so long as the facilities provided for each group were of equal value. In 1954 the Court found that:

> Segregation of white and colored children in public schools has a detrimental effect upon the colored children. The impact is greater when it has the sanction of the law, for the policy of separating the races is usually interpreted as denoting the inferiority of the negro group... We conclude that, in the field of public education, the doctrine of "separate but equal" has no place. Separate

jacket, which was widely reproduced and turned Andy Warhol into an instant fan. Each author used the other as the basis for a sexually transitive character in their novel: Capote becomes the effeminate Dill, and Lee turns into the tomboy Idabel in *Other Voices*.

In November, 1959, just after she finished *To Kill a Mockingbird*, Lee joined Capote on a trip to investigate a mysterious murder in Holcomb, Kansas. A prominent grain farmer, his wife and two teenage children had been bound, gagged and shot at close range. Capote was intrigued by the story, but his research was hampered by the locals' reaction to his somewhat camp New York manner. Lee's more down-to-earth curiosity and sympathy produced information more freely. She was also invaluable in cataloguing and storing their findings. *In Cold Blood* (1965), the book that finally emerged from this venture, was a pioneering work of fact/fiction. It made Capote's fortune ■

educational facilities are inherently unequal.

It is hard to exaggerate the shock of this decision in the South. First of all, its implications went far beyond education, since "separate but equal" was the principle on which the whole spread of Jim Crow legislation was grounded: racial segregation, not just in schools and colleges, but also on trains and buses, in hotels and restaurants, hospitals, parks and public meeting places (see p.26).

Secondly, the thought of blacks and whites together in school awoke that deep-seated southern fear – amounting almost to paranoia – of racial amalgamation through "intermarriage", code for interracial sex. If this link between the schoolroom and widespread miscegenation may seem far-fetched, consider Gunnar Myrdal's findings, in his monumental study of the southern mentality, that southerners considered "both that Negro men have a strong desire for 'intermarriage', and that white women would be open to proposals from Negro men *if* "they are not guarded from even meeting them on an equal plane". In fact, Myrdal takes the connection further, suggesting that the popular southern fear of interracial sex had been the basis for the whole apparatus of segregation, not just in education; it was "the principle around which the whole structure of segregation of the Negroes – down to disenfranchisement and denial of equal opportunities on the labor market –

Harper Lee and Truman Capote, 1966

[was] organized".

The fear of amalgamation would explain why it took so much legal pressure – again, running, all the way to the Supreme Court – for the University of Alabama at Tuscaloosa finally to admit an African-American woman called Autherine Lucy to do postgraduate work in Education – but forbade her the use of the university's dormitories and dining halls. Lucy, a modest, soft-spoken woman of 26, was welcomed by some undergraduates on campus, but on the night following the day she enrolled, the Ku Klux Klan burned a cross on the lawn of the black high school in Tuscaloosa. Three days later around a thousand male students demonstrated on campus against allowing Lucy to study there. Further unrest involving workers at a nearby rubber plant led the university authorities to ban her from campus (as they said) in the interests of public safety.

Meanwhile, on another segregation front, on December 1, 1955, Rosa Parks, sitting in a seat designated for whites on a bus in Montgomery, Alabama, refused to get up when a white passenger asked for it. Parks was arrested. On December 6 African Americans began to boycott the city's buses. As a result, since mainly blacks and poor whites used them, the city's buses lost around 90% of their revenue. Even so, it took a year and yet another ruling by the U. S. Supreme Court for the

WHAT IS A "JIM CROW LIBERAL"?

Malcolm Gladwell calls Atticus Finch a "Jim Crow liberal" for tolerating segregation temporarily in the hope that racial justice will evolve through the gradual enlightenment of ordinary people's hearts and minds, rather than through changes in the law.

A "liberal" in American usage is not a member of the political party dedicated to civil liberties, free trade and small government, but a person of slightly left-of-centre disposition: tolerant, open to new ideas, and un-ideological. The whole legal system of racial segregation in the South, in everything from education through transport down to drinking fountains in public parks was given the nickname "Jim Crow" after a character in an early 19th-century blackface

Montgomery transport authorities to back down. But the connection between segregation and sex came into really sharp focus on August 28, 1955, a little over a year after *Brown*. Emmett Till, a 14-year old African American from Chicago visiting relatives in Mississippi, went to buy candy in a country grocery store, where he is supposed to have flirted with – perhaps whistled at – a white woman, Carolyn Bryant, 21, in charge of the store at the time.

When she told her husband Roy, he was enraged, and went looking for Till with his half-brother J. W. Milam. When they found him at his

minstrel show – that is, a popular entertainment in which white actors blacked their faces to caricature African-American singers and dancers.

Jim Crow laws began to be enacted by southern states and local authorities as the initial force of Reconstruction after the Civil War began to subside. By the mid 1870s most of the segregationist rules were in place, eventually justified by the constitutional claim, tested in the U.S. Supreme Court in *Plessy v. Ferguson* (1896), that the facilities

offered blacks and whites were "separate but equal". Between 1890 and 1910, to buttress Jim Crow laws locally, most southern states introduced voting restrictions like literacy and comprehension tests, which had the effect of disenfranchising most African-Americans and incidentally many poor whites too. This is why the campaign to register southern African-Americans to vote was such an important part of the 1960s civil rights movement ∎

uncle's place, they dragged him out and took him to a barn, where they beat him around the face and body, gouging out an eye, then shot him through the head. Weighting the body down with a cotton gin fan, they then threw it in the Tallahatchie River. Soon arrested, Bryant and Milam were prosecuted for murder a month later. After a trial lasting just five days, the jury was sent out to consider their verdict. It took them just over an hour to acquit both defendants. "If we hadn't stopped for pop," said one juror afterwards, "it wouldn't have taken that long."

Within a year, now protected by double jeopardy, Bryant and Milam gave an interview to *Look* magazine, in which they admitted to having killed Till, showing no remorse for the act. Reaction to the Till murder had been hostile, even in Mississippi at first, but when the verdict came through and the boy's mother had his body brought back to Chicago, insisting on a public funeral with an open coffin showing that his murderers had done to his face, the outraged African-American community mobilised for action.

Black news magazines like *Jet* ran with the story; soon it spread to mainstream papers across the rest of the country, in time accelerated by the *Look* interview. Politicians became involved. William Faulkner published two searching essays in *Harpers* magazine in 1956. Langston Hughes and Gwendolyn Brooks wrote poems. Bob Dylan wrote and sang "The Death of Emmett Till". Congress passed the Civil Rights Act of 1957 allowing the U. S. Department of Justice to intervene in local law cases in which civil rights seemed in jeopardy.

If *Brown* laid the fire for the Civil Rights movement, Emmett Till's murder and its aftermath struck the match. When Rosa Parks was ordered to the "colored" seats at the back of that Montgomery bus, she almost complied, she said later, but then "I thought of Emmett Till and I just couldn't go back".

So how do these two notorious trials, separated by two decades, bear on *To Kill a Mockingbird*? Harper Lee has claimed that she did not have the Scottsboro events in mind when she wrote her novel. Answering Patrick Chura's queries, she "indicated that she was not in Mississippi and was not present at the Emmett Till trial". But both legal encounters produced enough reverberations to have infiltrated the author's imagination, even if only subliminally.

First, take the threat of the lynch mob, followed by the excited, carnival-like atmosphere in the Maycomb town square on the day Tom Robinson's trial is due to begin. The same happened in Scottsboro. Hollice Ransdall, a young teacher, journalist and activist who covered the scene for the American Civil Liberties Union (ACLU), reported: "People from surrounding counties and states began arriving by car and train with the coming of dawn." By ten o'clock "a crowd of 8,000 to 10,000 swarmed in the narrow village streets... packing the outside rim of the Square around the Courthouse with a solid mass of humanity".

A striking similarity between the novel and the first Scottsboro trial is the language used by the victims in describing the rapes: an odd mixture of heightened melodrama to express the assaults and

The jury for the Emmett Till trial, September 21 1955

primness to denote the act itself, prose reminiscent of sensational crime magazines like *The Police Gazette*. Here is Mayella's account:

> *Just run up behind me, he did. He got me round*
> *the neck, cussin' me and sayin' dirt –*
> *I fought'n'hollered, but he had me round the*
> *neck. He hit me agin an' agin... he chunked me on*
> *the floor an' choked me'n took advantage of me.*
> *(18)*

And here is Victoria Price's, in the second trial in 1933:

> It took three of them to hold me. One was holding
> my legs and the other had a knife
> to my throat while the other one ravished me.

This inauthentic language mirrors the deceitful motives of both accusers: Victoria's concern to avoid arrest under the Man Act, and Mayella's need to hide her own sexual advances towards Tom and her father's assault on her. As Judge Horton put it in his statement explaining why he was setting aside the verdict of the 1933 trial:

> "History, sacred and profane, and the common
> experience of mankind teach us that women of the
> character shown in this case are prone for selfish
> reasons to make false accusations both of rape and

of insult upon the slightest provocation for ulterior purposes."

More generally, the trial in the novel recapitulates features of both the historical trials. All three cases involve the explosive confrontation between what Patrick Chura calls the "dual icons of the 'black rapist'... [and] 'vulnerable and sacred' southern womanhood". As in Tom Robinson's case, both historical trials were heard by all-white, all-male juries hostile to the black interest, and in both the antagonists out to get the African American(s) were uneducated poor whites.

Chura goes on to suggest other features that tie Tom Robinson more specifically to the Till case. Both local communities despised the poor whites involved as "white trash"; both trials featured a fair-minded judge and a "courageous attorney" like Atticus. (One was Gerald Chatham, who did his best to prosecute Till's killers, albeit futilely.) In other words, by 1955 the tendency towards a more even-handed justice came as much from within the local community as from without. *To Kill a Mockingbird* reflects that (slightly) gentler tone.

How important is the narrator's age?

Near the beginning of the novel, that first summer when they first meet Dill, Scout tells us that Jem was "nearly ten" and she "almost six". At the beginning of Part Two, following the death of Mrs Dubose, Jem is 12 and Scout eight. Those remain their ages as that third summer gives way to the autumn of the trial and the novel's dénouement.

So there's no doubt about Scout's stated age. What we might call her rhetorical age is another matter. This is an eight-year-old who can say (of Aunt Alexandra's missionary circle): "Ladies in bunches always filled me with vague apprehension" (24). At seven she comes up with "A flip of the coin revealed the uncompromising lineaments of Aunt Alexandra and Francis" (9). A year younger and her vocabulary is revealed as, if anything, even more astounding, as she comments (of the children's amateur dramatics): "our repertoire was vapid from countless reproductions" (1). In other words, it's clear that at points like these her prose style keeps no company with her stated age.

Early reviewers, even those sympathetic to the novel, were a bit taken aback by this mismatch between Scout's stated and rhetorical age. "The story is seen through her eyes," wrote Edwin Bruell, "though what precocious eyes they sometimes are – like those of the son of the Lady Macduff." Phoebe Adams, who called the novel "pleasant, undemanding reading", had to admit that it was "frankly and completely impossible, being told in the first person by a six-year-old girl with the prose style of a well-educated adult". The more important question is whether Harper Lee makes Scout know any more than a girl of her age could. Or maybe, since it is difficult to disentangle knowing from saying, it would be more accurate to ask if she perceives or experiences things beyond her years. The answer is no. Adams admits that the author has "made an attempt to confine the information in the text to what Scout would actually know", but then claims that this effort is "no more than a casual gesture toward plausibility". This is quite wrong.

The first thing to get straight is that, within the action and as perceived by others in the story, Scout looks and acts like a little girl, albeit a precocious, tomboyish one. She feels bewildered and out of place on her first day at school. She fights with Walter Cunningham in the school yard. She rides inside an old tyre, and is childishly, superstitiously terrified when it bumps into the front steps of the Radley Place. She and Jem like to go hunting rabbits, squirrels and birds (though not mockingbirds, of course) with their air rifles.

Opposite: Mary Badham as Scout and Phillip Alford as Jem in the film of To Kill a Mockingbird, *released in 1962*

Within the action she talks like a little girl too. Here is the moment when she and Jem meet Dill:

> "I'm Charles Baker Harris," he said. "I can read."
>
> "So what?" I said.
>
> "I just thought you'd like to know I can read. You got anything needs readin' I can do it."
>
> "How old are you," asked Jem, "four-and-a-half?"
>
> "Goin' on seven."
>
> "Shoot, no wonder, then," said Jem, jerking his thumb at me. "Scout yonder's been readin' ever since she was born, and she ain't even started to

---

A CHILD'S PERSPECTIVE

Authors who want a child's perspective on adult themes in fiction have always got to find a way to draw out aspects of social and moral complexity beyond the child's comprehension. In

To Kill a Mockingbird Harper Lee makes Scout talk as a child when engaged in dialogue, but allows her an adult's vocabulary and range of perceptions when telling the story. In *What Maisie Knew* (1897), Henry James tackles the problem differently. He makes no attempt to mimic his little heroine's verbal repertoire, but uses his own highly complex prose style to dramatise the experience

*school yet. You look right puny for goin' on
seven."*

"I'm little but I'm old," he said...

*"Folks call me Dill," said Dill, struggling
under the fence.*

*"Do better if you go over it instead of under
it," I said. "Where'd you come from?" (1)*

This is engagingly accurate children's getting-to-
know-you dialogue, with accomplishments stated
up-front and emphasis on age as a badge of rank,
characteristically inflated with "goin' on". As Scout
tells it (and participates in it), it is entirely
naturalistic, exactly right for their ages.
Scout's reporting of dialogue retains its

appropriate to her years as
she ages throughout the
novel from around six to
early adolescence.

Maisie is the daughter of
divorced parents, Ida and
Beale Farrange, with each
of whom she lives for six
months at a time. The
parents remarry but
continue to have lovers
outside marriage, while
their new spouses start an
affair with each other. This
story line is confusing
enough for adult readers;

think how it must baffle the
(then) seven-year-old
Masie, as, while walking in
Hyde Park with her
stepfather Sir Claude, she
comes across her mother
arm in arm with a man she
has never seen before.

Her mother greets her
with effusive warmth:

*"My own child," Ida
murmured in a voice – a
voice of sudden confused
tenderness – that it seemed
to her she had heard for the*

authenticity in more complex exchanges too, as in those passages when an adult she respects – usually her father, but sometimes Calpurnia, among others – tries to explain something. In cases like these she reproduces the adult's speech apparently faithfully, as she hears it, even if she doesn't understand it completely, and retains her own child-like responses to it:

> "Scout, you aren't old enough to understand some things yet, but there's been some high talk around town to the effect that I shouldn't do much about defending this man. It's a peculiar case – it won't come to trial until summer session. John Taylor was kind enough to give us

first time... The next moment she was on her mother's breast, where, amid a wilderness of trinkets, she felt as if she had been thrust, with a smash of glass, into a jeweller's shop front, but only to be as suddenly ejected with a push and the brisk injunction: "Now go to the Captain!"

Maisie glanced at the gentleman submissively, but felt the want of more introduction. "The Captain?"

Sir Claude broke into a laugh. "I told her it was the Count."

Ida stared; she rose so superior that she was colossal. "You're too utterly loathsome," she then declared. "Be off!" she repeated to her daughter. Maisie stared, moved backward, and, looking at Sir Claude, "Only for a moment," she signed to him in her bewilderment.

But he was too angry to heed her – too angry with his wife; as she turned away she heard his anger a postponement..."

"If you shouldn't be defendin' him, then why are you doin' it?"

"For a number of reasons," said Atticus. "The main one is, if I didn't I couldn't hold up my head in town, I couldn't represent this county in the legislature, I couldn't even tell you or Jem not to do something again."

"You mean if you didn't defend that man, Jem and me wouldn't have to mind you any more?"

"That's about right." (9)

Atticus is talking about the authority that comes from the personal integrity gained and reinforced by doing his job – as a lawyer, a law-maker, a father

---

break out. "You damned old b----!" she couldn't quite hear all. It was enough, it was too much; she fled before it rushing even to a stranger for the shock of such a change of tone.

Through this almost surreal sequence of events, as baffling to the reader as it is to Maisie, the child makes her way by means of primary feelings: the physical feel of her mother's bejeweled bosom, and her emotional feel for reversals of mood, in Ida first embracing her, then suddenly pushing her away, and in Sir Claude's abrupt "change of tone". She knows nothing of the complex erotic dynamics of the grownups, or why their relationships seem to shift so rapidly. She is even too innocent to grasp the word Sir Claude uses for Ida, since when the Captain asks her what Sir Claude has called Ida, Maisie reports, "damned old brute" ▪

– but, true to her age, Scout's abstract vocabulary doesn't extend beyond the arena of the family. As it is, however, her relative naivety, mixed with a cunning eye for relaxing family discipline, brings the moral issue to a sharp point.

Much of the dialogue in *To Kill a Mockingbird* is like this, stripped of descriptive scaffolding. But not all. The following exchange is more problematic. It's the passage in which Scout and Jem tell Atticus and Aunt Alexandra about their visit to Calpurnia's church.

"You were all coming back from Calpurnia's church that Sunday?"

Jem said, "Yessum, she took us."

I remembered something. "Yessum, and she promised me I could come out to her house some afternoon, Atticus. I'll go next Sunday if it's all right, can I? Cal said she'd come get me if you were off in the car."

"You may not."

Aunt Alexandra said it. I wheeled around, startled, then turned back to Atticus in time to catch his swift glance at her, but it was too late. I said: "I didn't ask you!"

For a big man Atticus could get up and down from a chair faster than anyone I ever knew. He was on his feet, "Apologize to your aunt," he said.

"I didn't ask her, I asked you –"

Atticus turned his head and pinned me to the

wall with his good eye. His voice was deadly:
   "First, apologize to your aunt."
   "I'm sorry, Aunty," I muttered. (14)

Here again, the spoken words and their arrangement are naturalistically childlike, but now the direct speech is tagged by identifiers like "he said", "I muttered", the latter word already well beyond a child's vocabulary and level of sophistication, if only because of its self-reflective humour. Moreover the dialogue is interleaved with descriptions like "I wheeled around, startled, then turned back..." – a compound sentence with participial modifier, well beyond the syntactical repertoire of an eight-year-old, as Scout is by then.

The simple rule is that Scout's speech turns adult when she is talking to the reader, telling the story. While undertaking this narrative business she moves well beyond a child's story-telling capabilities. When setting a scene, or transitioning between one scene and another, or analysing the action, or drawing a conclusion, she is as adult and as educated as Harper Lee herself. Here she describes the court-house square on the day on which Tom Robinson's trial begins:

It was a gala occasion. There was no room at the public hitching rail for another animal, mules and wagons were parked under every available tree. The court-house square was covered with picnic parties sitting on newspapers, washing down biscuit and syrup with warm milk from fruit jars. Some people were gnawing on cold chicken and cold fried pork chops. The more affluent chased their food with drugstore Coca-Cola in bulb-shaped soda glasses. Greasy-faced children popped-the-whip through the crowd, and babies lunched at their mothers' breasts. (16)

There remain elements of childlike observation in this setting of the scene, but the whole is put together in an entirely adult way. It is partly to do with the syntax: the sophisticated use of participial constructions like "sitting on" and "washing down". Vocabulary comes into it too. Words like "affluent" and "gala" establish an adult perspective: the former conveying a sociological interest and the latter the overriding irony that would be lost on a child, that of a hanging as a holiday.

This degree of narrative sophistication does not conflict with what the child perceives, much less invalidate it. The crowded hitching rail, the varieties of food and drink on offer, the children popping the whip – all are details that a child might pick up. The strong but false impression that Scout perceives or experiences things beyond her years is due to the comment, the analysis, above all the contextualisation, that the authorial voice, still in Scout's first person, offers up to the primary experience.

There are simpler ways of establishing this ironic

tension between older awareness and younger naivety. In Charles Dickens's *Great Expectations* (1860 – 61) Mr Jaggers the lawyer reveals to Pip that he is destined to "come into a handsome property", but only after being taken from his loving brother-in-law (and father figure) Joe Gargery and "brought up as a gentleman – in a word, as a young fellow of great expectations". Pip is ecstatic: "My dream was out; my wild fancy was surpassed by sober reality; Miss Havisham was going to make my fortune on a grand scale."

As Jaggers stipulates each condition of the grant – that Pip should retain his nickname "Pip" and not Philip Pirrip, his baptised name; that he must never enquire into the identity of his benefactor – Pip assents with mounting excitement: "My heart was beating so fast, and there was such a singing in my ears, that I could scarcely stammer I had no objection...".

Pip's "wild fancy" remains just that. It is not that the wealthy, eccentric Miss Havisham is grooming him for her daughter Estella, with whom he has fallen in love; his true benefactor is someone both much truer and much less respectable. He breaks his apprenticeship, prepares to leave Joe and go to London, where the process of turning him into a fine gentleman will further alienate him from his family. But before moving on in the story, Pip the narrator reflects remorsefully on the moral implications of his folly:

*Oh dear good Joe, whom I was so ready to leave
and so unthankful to, I see you again, with your
muscular blacksmith's arm before your eyes, and
your broad chest heaving, and your voice dying
away. Oh dear good faithful tender Joe, I feel the
loving tremble of your hand upon my arm, as
solemnly this day as if it had been the rustle of an
angel's wing.*

Here the distinction between the young, naïve
Pip and his older, wiser self is not established
through linguistic difference, but through
analepsis, or flashback. What happens is that the
narrator moves into the future briefly, from which
(more experienced) perspective he can then
comment on the present action. But it's a
perspective that readers cannot yet share, since
they don't yet know the whole story – above all the
mystery of Pip's true benefactor.

Like Dickens, Harper Lee faced the challenge
of how to embed a naïve, yet fresh and engaging
child's point of view within a book for adults. Her
solution was linguistic: Scout talks like a child in
the action but like an adult when narrating that
action. Yet though Scout as child might notice
the raw elements – the people and events that
form the basis of the novel's complex social and
moral theme – the narrative needs Scout as
adult to give them meaning, to shape them and
put them in the context of Maycomb's social

and historical conventions.

But this is not an alien voice. It is Scout as an adult looking back on her childhood experience; it does not invade the consciousness of the child. The clearest clue that this is how to read the novel comes on the third page of the book, in the long description of Maycomb, that "old town", that "tired old town when I first knew it":

People moved slowly then. They ambled across the square, shuffled in and out of the stores around it, took their time about everything. A day was twenty-four hours long but seemed longer. There was no hurry, for there was nowhere to go, nothing to buy and no money to buy it with, nothing to see outside the boundaries of Maycomb County. (1)

It couldn't be clearer. That was then; the narrative voice is now. It is Scout grown up.

How does the first-person narrative work?

It is a critical commonplace, and also quite wrong, that Scout Finch is a 20th-century Huck Finn. They do have this in common: standing somewhat apart from their environments, both characters focus an innocent perspective on the faults and fallacies of their contemporary societies. Having seen through the conventional evil, they act for the good. But as narrators the two characters function very differently.

Mark Twain's *Adventures of Huckleberry Finn* (1884), one of the greatest (and funniest) of American novels, explores the cruelties and absurdities of the southern slave-holding system from the vantage point of a poor country boy lighting out from what he calls "sivilization", floating down the Mississippi River on a raft, together with a fugitive slave called Jim.

Huckleberry Finn starts off as a sequel to Mark Twain's *The Adventures of Tom Sawyer* (1876), at the end of which Tom and his friend Huck have inherited the ill-gotten booty of the murderous Injun Joe. Now that Huck has come into money, he must become respectable; so he is adopted by the Widow Douglas and her sister Miss Watson, "a tolerable slim old maid with goggles on".

Accustomed to sleeping in a sugar-hogshead and eating out of a barrel down in the town tanyard, Huck finds the decorum of town life – that is, bourgeois respectability – quite confining. In his new clothes "I couldn't do nothing but sweat and sweat, and feel all cramped up". As for meals at the widow's:

> *The widow rang a bell for supper, and you had to come to time. When you got to the table you*

couldn't go right to eating but you had to wait for the widow to tuck down her head and grumble a little over the victuals, though there warn't really anything the matter with them – that is, nothing only everything was cooked by itself. In a barrel of odds and ends it is different; things get mixed up and the juice kind of swaps around, and the things go better.

From this paragraph alone it should be obvious that Huck Finn is more like Walter Cunningham than Scout Finch. Huck is unused to regular meal times; he has never encountered the saying of grace before eating, or the separation of meat, potatoes and green vegetables on the plate. The comedy of this scene depends on how strange what we take as the ordinary conventions of mealtime must seem, as seen from outside the experience of "sivilization".

Scout is very different. She is from a "good background", and is familiar with these niceties of table manners, even if she doesn't always observe them. She is different in another way too. Huck's father, from whom he has to escape, is the town drunk who beats him and locks him in a cabin until he can get his hands on his money, and is later found naked, shot dead, in a derelict whorehouse floating down the Mississippi River. Scout's father is totally different: a strong role model, whose advice she seeks and takes. Above all, Scout has the superstructure of that "adult" register discussed in the preceding chapter.

As a child innocent of adult motives and concerns, Huck is a first-person narrator like Scout. But as an outlaw who prefers to live rough, affiliated to no part of the town's society, he is free of all social conventions, both emotionally and cognitatively. As the story progresses, his point of view remains "naïve", the fixed point of unwitting, radical satire throughout the book that bears his name.

Scout, on the other hand, has her roots in the town's society, and at its highest level. This is made quite explicit, by Jem and Aunt Alexandra to name just two. Jem's social plot of the town is a simple sketch:

> *"There's four kinds of folks in the world. There's the ordinary kind like us and the neighbors, there's the kind like the Cunninghams out in the woods, the kind like the Ewells down at the dump, and the Negroes." (23)*

In fact this hierarchy could be fleshed out a bit. Even among the whites, Maycomb has five distinct classes. There are the old, landed gentry of Finch's landing, a category that Aunt Alexandra is keen to reinforce because it distinguishes herself and her immediate family, including Atticus and his two children, from their immediate neighbours. Below them come the upper middle class, comprising Maudie, the members of Aunt Alexandra's missionary society and the professionals like Dr Reynolds and Judge Taylor. Then come the middle class, people in trade, like Braxton Bragg Underwood, owner-editor of the Maycomb *Tribune*, and Sam Levy, who supposedly faced down the Klan by reminding them that he had sold them the sheets on their backs.

Below them are what the Victorians used to call the deserving poor, like the Cunninghams of Old Sarum, who, as Atticus puts it, "hadn't taken anything from or off of anybody since they migrated to the New World" (23). At the bottom are the Ewells, the undeserving poor, or in southern American terms, white trash.

At times Scout bridles at Aunt Alexandra's snobbish insistence on the Maycomb caste system, but she has to admit that her "theory had something behind it". Furthermore it is reinforced by her respected father. Here he is speaking sternly to Jem:

"Your aunt has asked me to try and impress upon you and Jean Louise that you are not from run-of-the-mill people, that you are the product of several generations' gentle breeding –"
Atticus paused, watching me locate an elusive redbug on my leg.
"Gentle breeding," he continued, when I had

found and scratched it, "and that you should try to live up to your name." (13)

The tone is nicely balanced here: Aunt Alexandra's message, which Atticus delivers under pressure, is interrupted by Scout's itchy redbug. Scout finds Aunt Alexandra's class system too complex. Later, when Jem outlines his "four kinds of folks", she answers: "Naw, Jem, I think there's just one kind of folks. Folks." This makes Jem very angry: "That's what I thought too," he said at last, "When I was your age. If there's just one kind of folks, why can't they get along with each other?" (23). He has a point.

"WHITE TRASH"

As so often with popular prejudices – racism is another example – a "scholarly" view paralleled and added support to the belief that white trash were degenerate by nature. When the likes of Erskine Caldwell and Margaret Mitchell were writing about white trash in the 1930s, the "science" of eugenics enjoyed enormous prestige in Europe and America. This was the belief that the mental and physical powers of the human stock could and should be improved by selective breeding.

Americans were particularly drawn to the study because it seemed to solve a problem with the prestigious theory of biological determinism, the hierarchy of immigrants that ran from the "Anglo-Saxon" and "Nordic" settlers at the top,

For all that, Scout is no revolutionary, nor is she alienated from her family and from conventional society, as Huck Finn is. She does not react against her class. Where she differs from others in Maycomb, apart from her ambiguous gender, is in her age – a difference that Jem often uses to put her down – and her natural inquisitiveness.

Do Scout's age and curiosity make up a point of view that challenges the social conventions of Mayscomb? Not "challenge", exactly, but maybe confront, certainly critique. A good example is the way she reports the meeting of Aunt Alexandra's missionary circle. "Ladies in bunches always filled me with vague apprehension," the adult voice

through the "Alpine" and "Mediterranean" peoples in the middle, down to the blacks of African origin at the bottom of the pile. The problem was that the most famously deprived and backward peoples, like the hillbillies of the Appalachian Mountains, the country poor of Oklahoma and the sharecroppers in the South, were white, native born Americans of "Anglo-Saxon" stock. The only way to explain this contradiction was to show that these families had degenerated over time through excessive interbreeding.

Accordingly, from 1910 the Eugenics Records Office (ERO) had been sending fieldworkers out to gather data to "prove" that the poverty, sexual promiscuity and cultural backwardness of the marginal country poor were all "cacogenic" traits, the result of many generations of degeneration through inbreeding. Hence the hare lip, the feeblemindedness, "they couldn't help it", "it was in their blood", and so on ▪

recalls, using a child's noun – "bunches" – to ground the scene in her youthful feelings. Much of the scene moves through Scout's deadpan rendering of the prejudices and long-distance concerns of the ladies' missionary zeal:

> *From the kitchen I heard Mrs Grace Merriweather giving a report in the living room on the squalid lives of the Mrunas, it sounded like to me. They put the women out in huts when their time came, whatever that was; they had no sense of family – I knew that'd distress Aunty – they subjected children to terrible ordeals when they were thirteen; they were crawling with yaws and earworms, they chewed up and spat out the bark of a tree into a communal pot and then got drunk on it. Immediately thereafter, the ladies adjourned for refreshments. (24)*

Distant Africans may invite Mrs Merriweather's concern, but her empathy for Africans closer to home is decidedly limited. It is she who remarks to Mrs Farrow (and in Calpurnia's hearing): "Gertrude, I tell you, there's nothing more distracting than a sulky darky." The irony takes its cue from Dickens's Mrs Jellyby in *Bleak House* (1852–53), whose "telescopic philanthropy" for an obscure African tribe diverts her attention from the chaos in her own household.

For Scout just to juxtapose Mrs Merriweather's

remarks, either in paraphrase or by direct quotation, is sufficient comment, but it's important to note that although the point of view may be that of a child (she doesn't know what "when their time came" means, for instance), narrative phrases in her paraphrase, like "subjected children to terrible ordeals", are adult.

Not all of Scout's childlike observations function as satire. At times her curiosity leads her to receive wisdom in a response delivered by, say, Calpurnia or Atticus. After she discovers Miss Caroline's ignorance of her pupils' home life and her suspicion of Scout's ability to write, Scout wants to leave school:

"You never went to school and you do all right, so I'll just stay home too. You can teach me like Grandaddy taught you 'n' Uncle Jack."

"No I can't," said Atticus. "I have to make a living. Besides, they'd put me in jail if I kept you at home – dose of magnesia for you tonight and school tomorrow."

"I'm feeling all right, really."

"Thought so. Now what's the matter?"

Bit by bit I told him the day's misfortunes.

"– and she said you taught me all wrong, so we can't ever read any more, ever. Please don't send me back, please sir."

Atticus stood up and walked to the edge of the porch. When he completed his examination of the wisteria vine he strolled back to me.

"First of all," he said, "if you can learn a simple trick, Scout, you'll get along a lot better with all kinds of folks. You never really understand a person until you consider things from his point of view."

"Sir?"

" – until you climb into his skin and walk around in it."

Atticus said I had learned many things today, and Miss Caroline had learned several things herself. (3)

Here there is a clear distinction between the child's and the adult's understanding, as configured in the dialogue between Scout and Atticus, yet the grown-up Scout is still involved in the narrative, as when she portrays Atticus, challenged by the child's candid logic, playing for time by walking over to examine the wisteria. This is not a tactic a child would recognise.

What Scout has learned, from her father rather than her teacher, is of course tolerance, or at least the imaginative exercise that encourages it. It is this thought process that will lead her to understand why Atticus is defending Tom Robinson, and – even more remarkably – to sympathise with Mayella Ewell:

As Tom Robinson gave his testimony, it came to

me that Mayella Ewell must have been the
loneliest person in the world. She was even
lonelier than Boo Radley, who had not been out
of the house in twenty-five years. When Atticus
asked had she any friends, she seemed not to
know what he meant, then she thought he was
making fun of her. She was as sad, I thought, as
what Jem called a mixed child: white people
wouldn't have anything to do with her because
she lived among pigs; Negroes wouldn't have
anything to do with her because she was white.
She couldn't live like Mr. Dolphus Raymond,
who preferred the company of Negroes, because
she didn't own a river-bank and she wasn't from
a fine old family. (19)

In feeling for Mayella, the least attractive
character in the novel – indeed, in bridging the
widest class gap in the story – Scout has certainly
learned Atticus's lesson. But her sympathy is far
from naïve, reinforced as it is by her astute class
analysis that land ownership and a respectable
genealogy can overtrump even miscegenation.

When she thinks of Mayella's loneliness, Scout
recalls Boo Radley. As compared to her feelings for
Mayella, her understanding of Boo Radley takes
the whole novel to develop. Boo haunts the rest of
the action – not as a ghost (the children's early
fear) but as a persistent thought in Scout's mind.
And whereas her sympathy for Mayella can do the

girl no good at all, Scout's understanding of Boo evolves into a redemptive force.

Maycomb's view of the Radleys is a bundle of ignorant suspicions: a phantom leaves the house at night and peers into people's windows, or breathes on their azaleas to freeze them, or tears their chickens apart. African Americans will not pass the house on the sidewalk, but cross the street and whistle. Pecans falling from the Radley trees into the schoolyard go ungathered, because everyone knows that Radley pecans would kill you. (1)

As a young child Scout is not immune to these rumours, but it's significant that when the children dream up their various excursions on to Radley territory, it is Jem and Dill in the lead, with Scout trailing behind. It is she who first finds one of Boo's gifts in the knothole, and dares to go back and collect it. It is two sticks of gum, which she chews, until Jem forces her not just to spit it out, but also to gargle with antiseptic. As more gifts emerge, starting with the two polished Indian-head pennies, Jem begins to take an interest.

By the middle of her story Boo Radley is no longer a phantom to Scout, or any kind of supernatural presence, but a sad human being arousing her concern and curiosity:

> "Dill?"
> "Mm?"
> "Why do you reckon Boo Radley's never run off?"

Gregory Peck as Atticus Finch and Brock Peters as Tom Robinson in the 1962 film

*Dill signed a long sigh and turned away from me.
"Maybe he doesn't have anywhere to run off to..."*
(14)

Near the end of the novel, the Radley place has
long ceased to terrify her, but objectively, even
stripped of all superstitious associations, it is "no
less gloomy, no less chilly under its great oaks, and
no less uninviting". Now that she perceives the
reality of the Radley household, and her curiosity
has matured into sympathetic imagination, she
sometimes felt a twinge of remorse at ever having
taken part in what must have been sheer torment
for Arthur Radley – what reasonable recluse wants

children peeping through his shutters, delivering greetings on the end of a fishing pole, wandering in his collards at night?

There's a new note of formality here, signaled by Scout referring to Boo by his proper first name. With some dignity Scout takes Boo by the hand and leads him home, after Boo has carried Jem home, and saved their lives. It is a solemn procession, but it's fitting that she should be part of it, since it is she who comes closest to understanding the human truth of the Radley household.

So how does the first-person point of view function in *To Kill a Mockingbird*? The first thing to establish is that the character on whom it's based develops throughout the story, not just through experience but also by explicit teaching: lessons taught by Calpurnia, Jem and, above all, Atticus. Scout's curiosity and her innocent outlook that either questions prejudice or simply doesn't feel it allows her to engage with the social outcast, as Huck's does with Jim the runaway slave. Unlike Huck's case, though, Scout's narrative is often interlaced with those adult phrases, like "subjected children to terrible ordeals", or those adult ironies, like Atticus examining the wisteria, or her adult powers of class analysis.

In addition to her youth and curiosity, Scout's powers of observation and empathy depend on her unassailable class status. It gives her the security to be different, an inquiring child, sometimes a nuisance, without arousing hostility or outright rejection. Through her father, brother and surrogate mother her secure family life provides her still centre, her refuge, her role models and her education. And – though this is never shown in the story, since it must have come later – her class status provides her further, more formal education, which in turn reinforces and informs her powers of social analysis and her imaginative empathy.

But these powers grow so seamlessly that it's not possible to tell, for example, at what point she felt the sympathy for Mayella or the remorse for their treatment of Boo. The past tense of "It came to me" or "I sometimes felt" doesn't necessarily locate these feelings at the point of the action. They could be part of that integrating analysis provided by the confident adult voice so interwoven with the narrative.

Why is Scout a tomboy?

Tomboys, or girls who dress, act and behave as boys, are a popular feature of English and American children's fiction. Ruth ("Nancy") Blackett in Arthur Ransome's *Swallows and Amazons* series (1930 and following) "captains" a sailing dinghy, wears red trousers and a pirate's cap and says things like "shiver me timbers". In *Five on a Treasure Island* (1942), the first of Enid Blyton's

Famous Five stories – there were 21 of them in all – Georgina ("call me George") is 11, wears her hair short, and dresses like a boy. In between, chronologically speaking, is the American *Caddie Woodlawn* (1936), by Carol Ryne Brinks, set on the Wisconsin frontier in the 1860s, where 11-year-old Caroline ("Caddie") of the title lives with her family. Allowed to run free for her health, Caddie leads her brothers on all sorts of adventures in the surrounding woods, and even befriends a Native American tribe, whom she warns of a sneak attack by white settlers.

For older readers, tomboys have tended to be an all-American venture. One of the earliest was Josephine ("Jo") March in *Little Women* (1868 – 69), by Louisa May Alcott. Aged 15, Jo is the second of four sisters living with their mother in a small New England town, based on Concord, Massachusetts, where the author's family lived. Their father is away, having volunteered as a chaplain in the Civil War, and Jo wishes she could go too, but meanwhile has to make the most of domestic life, helping her mother and sisters to make ends meet. Jo is strong-minded, hot-tempered and awkwardly mannish, but she is also resourceful and loyal to her family. She aspires to be an author, writing plays for her sisters to perform and spending hours alone reading when she can be spared from the household chores. Louisa Alcott's father, Bronson, was an innovative educator and one of the transcendentalist philosophers, who believed in the inherent goodness of man when in direct touch with nature and not subservient to institutionalised religion and education; so his daughter's stories were likely to be open to progressive themes. Seen first as a story about and for teenage girls coming of age, then as a work of local colour about family life in New England, *Little Women* has been read more recently as an early feminist work, in that it explores the limits to a young woman's independence within the domestic and social constraints of the time.

Tomboys moved down South with the novels of Carson McCullers. Though centred on the lonely life of the deaf mute John Singer in a Georgia mill town, *The Heart is a Lonely Hunter* (1940) includes the tomboy Mick Kelly as one of his acquaintances. Twelve years old at the beginning of the story, Mick wears khaki shorts, a blue shirt, and tennis shoes and aspires to run faster and climb higher than any boy her age.

As she matures into a tall, raw-boned young woman and enters vocational college, where the gender roles are more rigidly reinforced than in her earlier schooling, she has to come to terms with dances and parties. Attracted to her next door neighbour, Harry Minowitz, by his strong political opinions, Mick falls in love for the first time. An adolescent sexual encounter leaves them both bewildered and unhappy, with the result that Mick retreats into her "inner room" to realise her musical compositions and to work on her dream of owning a piano.

A tomboy takes centre stage in McCullers's *The Member of the Wedding* (1946), a crucial source for *Mockingbird.* She is Frances ("Frankie") Addams, also 12 years old. Though in the third person, the narrative is from Frankie's point of view, in what is known technically as the free indirect style. Frankie's mother died giving birth to her, and her father is a remote figure, seldom in the story's frame. Her chief company are the family cook, Berenice Sadie Brown, and John Henry West, her six-year-old cousin.

The story covers a few days in a small southern town, late in summer when Frankie stopped being a member of anything. Too tall – "almost a big freak" – to be a little girl, she was still too young to be one of the big girls who were "thirteen, fourteen and even 15 years old", who " had this club, [of which] she was not a member".

As plans crystallise for her older brother's wedding, Frankie fantasises that at least she can be a member of that – not just to be a bridesmaid but to travel with the newlyweds on their honeymoon, accompanying them to somewhere snowy and cool, like Alaska. When the married couple leave without her, she is devastated. Returned home, she tries to run away, but then realises she doesn't know how to jump a freight train. At length a policeman tracks her down in a bar where she has had an earlier encounter with a lonely soldier, innocent on her part but harrowing nonetheless.

Tomboy novels raise the issue "that the categories available to women for racial, sexual and gendered identification are simply inadequate", according to Judith Halberstam. "In her novel McCullers shows this inadequacy to be a direct result of the tyranny of language – a structure that fixes people and things in place artificially but securely."

Frankie Addams reacts to this pressure by changing her name twice, from her baptismal Frances to the tomboyish Frankie, then – as she begins to live the fancy of maturing into a true lady for the wedding – F. Jasmine Addams. "Frankie thinks that naming represents the power of definition," Halberstam continues, "and name changing confers the power to reimagine identity, place, relation and even gender."

For Berenice the key variable is race. In her paradise:

"the world of the Holy Lord God... there would be no separate colored people in the world, but all human beings would be light brown color with blue eyes and black hair. There would be no colored people and no white people to make the colored people feel cheap and sorry all through their lives."

TEN FACTS ABOUT
TO KILL A MOCKINGBIRD

1.

To Kill a Mockingbird is required reading in three-quarters of all American high schools, second only in set-text status to *The Adventures of Huckleberry Finn*.

2.

In 1991, a Library of Congress survey found that *To Kill a Mockingbird* was second only to the Bible in readers' ranking of books that had made a difference to their lives.

3.

The American novelist Truman Capote, Lee's childhood friend and the model for Dill in the novel, was once thought largely to have written *To Kill a Mockingbird*. Documentary evidence later proved this rumour false.

Lee helped him to research *In Cold Blood*, which documented the brutal 1959 murder of a family from Kansas, playing an important role in gaining the trust of those who spoke to them. A resident recalls: "Nelle sort of managed Truman, acting as his guardian or mother. She broke the ice for him ." Another said of Capote: "he wasn't the kind of person I wanted to spend time with – he was very, very strange." Lee commented that "those people had never seen anyone like Truman – he was like someone coming off the moon."

4.

Though normally reluctant to comment on racial matters, President Obama introduced a re-mastered version of the movie on April 5, 2012, the film's 50th anniversary, with some of the original actors. Harper Lee, who seldom responds to events or approaches relating to the work, sent a message of appreciation.

5.

At the age of 100 Alice Lee, Harper's sister, was still practising the law in Monroeville in 2012. In the bank vault downstairs from her office is the original manuscript of *To Kill a Mockingbird*. The book is dedicated to Alice, "in consideration of Love and Affection".

6.

The book has been adapted as a play by Christopher Sergel. It opened in 1990 in Monroeville, Alabama and runs every May in the grounds of the courthouse. Townspeople make up the cast. White male audience members are chosen at the intermission to make up the jury. During the courtroom scene the play moves into the Monroe County Courthouse and the audience is racially segregated.

7.

Gregory Peck met Harper Lee's father, the model for Atticus, before the filming. A.C. Lee had once defended two black men accused of murdering a white storekeeper. Both clients, a father and son, were hanged. Lee's father died before the film's release, and Lee herself was so impressed by Peck's performance that she gave him her father's pocket watch, which he had with him the evening he was awarded the Oscar for best actor. It was Peck's first and only Oscar. Lee remains close to Peck's family, and Peck's grandson, Harper Peck Voll, is named after her.

8.

To Kill a Mockingbird was banned by Virginia Hanover County School Board in 1966 because it covered the subject of rape; Harper Lee defended her book, arguing that it embodied an honourable code of conduct and Christian ethic:

"Recently I have received echoes down this way of the Hanover County School Board's activities, and what I've heard makes me wonder if any of its members can read.

Surely it is plain to the simplest intelligence that "To Kill a Mockingbird" spells out in words of seldom more than two syllables a code of honor and conduct, Christian in its ethic, that is the heritage of all Southerners. To hear that the novel is "immoral" has made me count the years between now and 1984, for I have yet to come across a better example of doublethink.

I feel, however, that the problem is one of illiteracy, not Marxism. Therefore I enclose a small contribution to the Beadle Bumble Fund that I hope will be used to enroll the Hanover County School Board in any first grade of its choice."

9.
Harper Lee uses all three of her mother's names, Frances Cunningham Finch, in *To Kill a Mockingbird*.

10.
Robert Duvall made his film debut playing Boo Radley in 1962. To prepare for the role, Duvall spent six weeks out of the sun so that he would look the part of a person who has spent most of his life locked in a basement.

For these characters, "and for characters throughout McCullers's work", writes McKay Jenkins, "heaven is a place where identity, particularly racial and gender identity, is fluid, changeable, amorphous".

When *To Kill a Mockingbird* made its debut, McCullers wrote to a cousin to say, "Well, honey, one thing we know is that she's been poaching on my literary preserves." Reviewers couldn't avoid comparing the two books. Scout Finch is "the most appealing child since Carson McCullers's Frankie got left behind at the wedding", proclaimed *Time* Magazine for August 1, 1960. "After all," wrote Katherine Gauss Jackson, "we had *Member of the Wedding* not so long ago, with... the Negro cook in the kitchen so earthily wise in answering difficult questions when parents are not at hand. And here it all is again, but different."

The main difference lay in what Harper Lee brought to these "literary preserves". In *To Kill a Mockingbird* the issue of race concerns everyone, not just the African-American family cook. Furthermore, barriers of race and gender are linked even more systematically than in *The Member of the Wedding*. Roughly speaking, those who comply with the one also enforce the other. Conversely, those who question the racial barrier also challenge the social construction of gender. Aunt Alexandra is one of the enforcers. Scout remembers her as

*fanatical on the subject of my attire. I could not
possibly hope to be a lady if I wore breeches;
when I said I could do nothing in a dress, she said
I wasn't supposed to be doing things that
required pants. Aunt Alexandra's vision of my
deportment involved playing with small stoves,
tea sets, and wearing the Add-a-Pearl necklace
she gave me when I was born. (9)*

When she arrives to stay, seemingly forever, Aunt
Alexandra's first two utterances are her
preemptory order to Calpurnia, "Put my bag in the
front bedroom", and her brusque "Jean Louise,
stop scratching your head". Now that she's
established in the Finch household, she intends to
put an end to Scout's tomboyism: "We decided that
it would be best for you to have some feminine
influence," she tells Scout, ignoring her tomboy
name. "It won't be many years, Jean Louise, before
you become interested in clothes and boys" (13).
She also objects strenuously to Atticus's defence
of Tom.

   As Gary Richards points out, the true foil to
Aunt Alexandra is Miss Maudie: fully qualified in
the breeding and deportment that constitutes
southern womanhood, but unconventionally
manly in dress and daily behaviour and open-
minded to events in the outside world. She is also
much more flexible as to race, and supports
Atticus's defence of Tom.

In his seminal essay, Richards identifies a series of parodic relationships that "function to establish heterosexuality as existing in the novel primarily in comic deviations from its fictional norm". First, in the order of the story, there is Little Chuck Little's chivalric rescue of Miss Caroline from Burris Ewell's nits. When her screams bring the entire class to attention, Little Chuck "grinned broadly. 'There ain't no need to fear a cootie, ma'am. Now don't you be afraid, you just go back to your desk and teach us some more'" (3).

Then there is the unmarried Uncle Jack, with his loud mock courtship of Miss Maudie every Christmas:

We saw Uncle Jack every Christmas, and every Christmas he yelled across the street for Miss Maudie to come marry him. Miss Maudie would yell back, "Call a little louder, Jack Finch, and they'll hear you at the post office." Jem and I thought this a strange way to ask a lady's hand in marriage, but then Uncle Jack was rather strange. (5)

Next comes Jem's enforced reading to Mrs Dubose, an encounter, says Richards, "firmly within romantic expression" because although he brings no sonnets to the occasion, Jem reads from *Ivanhoe*, "a novel emblematic of romanticization of heterosexual courtship".

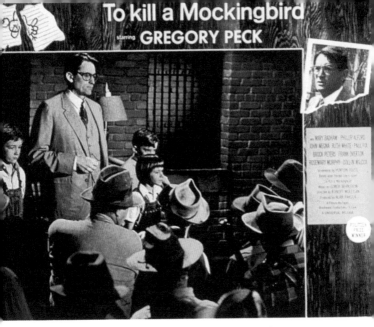

A poster for the 1962 film. Lee called the film a "work of art"

As the protagonist, Scout has two such mock heterosexual relationships, one with Dill Harris and the other with Boo Radley. Dill and Scout are the right age for each other, and indeed plan to get married, as she tells Francis, Alexandra's nasty grandson. He hoots with incredulity – "You mean that little runt Grandma says stays with Miss Rachel every summer?... I know all about him" – before going on to call Atticus a "nigger-lover" who "mortif[ies] the rest of the family" (9).

But as their first meeting makes clear Dill really is small; he looks four and a half but is seven years old. Not only that, but he wears sissy clothes, with his "blue linen shorts that buttoned to his shirt", instead of the overalls favoured by the town's boys. Dill is based on the real-life Truman Capote, the openly gay author who was Harper Lee's childhood friend in Monroeville. "Lee drew heavily upon Capote's effeminate childhood identity," continues Richards, "as he readily acknowledged."

All four of these relationships are disqualified by age, or sexual orientation, or the lack of mutual attraction. The only real heterosexual action in the novel is Tom's rape of Mayella, and even that is a fiction. Yet for all that, they provide more companionship, or exhibit more charity, or provide more mutual learning and development, than

TO KILL A MOCKINGBIRD AND CHILDREN'S FICTION

Writing to her friend, the Alabama novelist Caroline Ivey, in August 1961, Flannery O'Connor commented: "It's interesting that all the folks that are buying it don't know they're reading a child's book." O'Connor's remark wasn't meant as a compliment. By this time, "all the folks" reading the novel already numbered more than half a million, and just four months earlier Harper Lee had won the Pulitzer Prize for fiction, which O'Connor had coveted for herself.

Around the time *Mockingbird* was written the academic field of American studies was establishing itself in great generic sweeps across the nation's literature. What everyone agreed was that above all American writing those other, more conventional relationships in the book, the marriages of Mr and Mrs Merriweather, and especially of Aunt Alexandra and Uncle Jimmy.

The most serious of these parodic pairings, the only one that is neither satiric nor comic in some other sense, is Scout's with Boo Radley. Although their long series of non-encounters can hardly be called a courtship, on Scout's part it does at least involve her holding back from the boys' raids on the Radley house, and on Boo's part the offer of gifts in the old oak tree.

This pairing is undercut by disparities in age

---

had to be different from European, especially English literature, for otherwise what made it American?

But people differed on what this great American difference would be. According to Richard Chase in his *The American Novel and its Tradition* (1957), great American fiction would resemble the romance more than the novel. Instead of paying close attention to class and the social setting, American fiction would pit an isolated hero against the forces of nature. If the European novel was about

character, the American equivalent would be all about action in a melodramatic story line.

That was only half right, thought Leslie Fiedler. In his *Love and Death in the American Novel* (1960), the crucial difference is that great works of American fiction are "innocent, unfallen in a disturbing way". They are "notoriously at home in the children's section of the library, their level of sentimentality precisely that of a pre-adolescent". Though "experts on and status, and also by something of a gender reversal, as when, after saving the children's lives, Boo asks Scout if she will take him home. Yet the whole scene is worth quoting here:

> *"Will you take me home?" He almost whispered it, in the voice of a child afraid of the dark. I put my foot on the top step and stopped. I would lead him through our house, but I would never lead him home.*
>
> *"Mr. Arthur, bend your arm down here, like that. That's right, sir."*
>
> *I slipped my hand into the crook of his arm.*

indignity and assault, on loneliness and terror", great American works of fiction are childlike in the sense that they avoid the central subject of the European novel, "the passionate encounter of a man and woman".

Without love between the sexes, the American novel is forced "to choose between the two archetypes of innocent homosexuality and unconsummated incest; the love of comrades and that of brother and sister... Both themes are juvenile and regressive."

So it would be tempting to say that if *To Kill a Mockingbird* is a children's book, it rests squarely in a great tradition of national fiction – at least as projected by these founding theorists of American literature. This would be wrong. As for Chase's argument that American fiction tended toward romance, it is clear that Harper Lee was doing everything possible to steer clear of romance. The evidence of the book itself, with its naturalistic dialogue and its presentation of ordinary

*He had to stoop down a little to accommodate
me, but if Miss Stephanie Crawford was
watching from her upstairs window, she would
see Arthur Radley escorting me down the
sidewalk, as any gentleman would do. (31)*

"As any gentleman would do" sets the scene in the
context of a courtly romance, but it's important
that the scene is being set for Miss Stephanie
Crawford, the town gossip who has stirred up so
many rumours about Boo, and claims once to have
seen him outside her window staring in. So Scout
is not just showing her affection and respect for

people involved in everyday events, suggests it is unquestionably a work of literary realism.

The book also resists Fiedler's critique, to some extent. Though there is something in the fellowship of Scout, Jem and Dill to resemble the buddy love of Hawkeye and Chingachgook in *The Last of the Mohicans* or Huck and Jim in *The Adventures of Huckleberry Finn*, Captain Ahab, the demonic motivator of *Moby Dick*, and Henry Fleming undergoing his rite of passage in *The Red Badge of Courage*, have no equivalents in *To Kill a Mockingbird*.

If there is no seduction, love and marriage in *To Kill a Mockingbird*, the novel is scarcely without other adult themes. Yet there is some truth in Flannery O'Connor's judgement that it is a children's book – if only in the uncomplicated, un-displaced sense that it's about children and their development, and (thanks to the consensus of educators) read mainly by teenagers as part of their school or college curriculum ∎

Boo. By her masquerade of a heterosexual courtship Scout reclaims Boo from all those rumours and imputations around his solitary way of life.

So why is Scout a tomboy? Generally tomboys in fiction are a way of getting back at the system. There is something subversive, even transgressive, in granting to girls the same freedom and mobility and range of control allowed to boys, an imaginative flattening out of the normal hierarchy that appeals to the reader's sense of adventure. Tomboys can also be a way of exploring in fiction the limits of socially constructed gender. Judith Halberstam says that tomboyism is punished when

> it appears to be the sign of extreme male identification (taking a boy's name or refusing girl clothing of any type) and when it threatens to extend beyond childhood and into adolescence... We could say that tomboyism is tolerated as long as the child remains prepubescent; as soon as puberty begins, however, the full force of gender conformity descends on the girl.

Scout is spared this come-uppance, partly because the story ends before she reaches puberty, and partly because she makes tactical concessions to convention from time to time, as when she dresses up in her "pink Sunday dress, shoes, and a petticoat" when Aunt Alexandra's missionary circle comes to call, and when asked whether she wants to grow up to be a lawyer, answers, "'Nome, just a lady'"(24).

In any case – and unlike Carson McCullers – Harper Lee made Scout a tomboy for more positive reasons than to explore the anxieties of girls growing up. Scout's uncertain gender assignment unlocks her from conventional relationships and behaviour outside the family. She is the means by which Lee can question conventional society, even to the point of undermining conventional ways of doing and seeing things, including marriage. Freed from alliances, from prejudices and preconceptions, Scout can function as a stand-in for the author, as a neutral observer. More importantly, she can be the bringer of redemptive sympathy.

How good a lawyer is Atticus Finch?

"No real life lawyer has done more for the self-image or public perception of the legal profession than the hero of Harper Lee's novel, *To Kill a Mockingbird*," writes Steven Lubet, Professor of Law at Northwestern University:

> For nearly four decades, the name of Atticus Finch has been invoked to defend and inspire lawyers, to rebut lawyer jokes, and to justify (and fine tune) the

adversary system. Lawyers are greedy. What about Atticus Finch? Lawyers only serve the rich. Not Atticus Finch. Professionalism is a lost ideal. Remember Atticus Finch.

Professor Lubet leads what might be called the "real life" school of Atticus analysis, those who assess his legal performance as though it had really occurred in history, instead of within a novel. But real life, unlike art, often has rough edges. Which is why, for all his praise of the lawyer's nobility, Lubet does have one nagging question: did he bully Mayella Ewell during the course of his cross examination of her?

As Lubet points out, in the 1930s as in the 1950s, the dates of the novel's setting and composition, the standard defence against a rape charge was that the victim had consented in the act. Atticus did not merely raise the issue of consent. "Rather, he used a specific form of the defense that can be particularly offensive in both cases of the word. Let's call it the 'she wanted it' defense."

With no medical evidence that Mayella had been raped, Atticus makes great play of the assertion that Mayella's bruises on her right arm and the right side of her face could not possibly have been made by Tom Robinson, whose left arm had been immobilised after being caught in a cotton gin when he was a boy. But, as Lubet points out, Mayella's injuries could have been caused by a back-hand blow from Tom's right hand. Tom was a manual laborer, a powerful man, whose "powerful shoulders rippled under his thin shirt", according to Scout (18).

So Atticus must discredit the witness, suggesting that she planned to seduce Tom, getting her siblings out of the way by saving nickels for a year in order to send them off to town to buy ice creams. Tom testified that Bob Ewell's first words on entering the house were "You goddam whore,

Gregory Peck and Harper Lee on the set of the 1962 film

I'll kill ya!" Why would he say that if Tom was raping her? "The advocate's job is to provide the jury with reasons for acquittal," writes Professor Lubet:

> Atticus Finch gave his jury at least five separate justifications for believing that Mayella "wanted it." She lied, he told them, perhaps in fantasy, or out of spite, or in shame, or as a result of sexual frustration, or maybe just because she was confused.

In his gratuitous attack on Mayella Ewell, according to Lubet, Atticus takes his cue from Samuel Leibowitz's verbal assault on the two alleged victims in the Scottsboro case. In Victoria Price's case there *was* medical evidence, and it proved that she had had consensual intercourse some 24 hours before the alleged rape – in other words, that no rape had occurred as charged. But the defence did not stop there. "Victoria Price and Ruby Bates were portrayed as... promiscuous tramps at best, more likely prostitutes," Lubet writes. In the first retrial, it got worse:

> Victoria Price had to endure Samuel Leibowitz's ferocious cross-examination, which was described by one reporter as "the shredding of her life with a patient scalpel". Price had committed adultery and prostitution; she "treated" with black men; she

traded sex for liquor, favors, money, food, companionship, and love... The assault on Victoria Price was made all the more brutal by the fact that it was designed solely to degrade her, and not to develop any evidence actually relevant to the case. The defense, after all, was that the alleged intercourse had never occurred.

"Advocates will use the tools they have," adds Lubet. They will play on the jury's prejudices if it serves their client's case. Atticus was a decent man, honourable, courageous. His use of the "she wanted it defense" against Mayella, Lubet writes, means that he "was able to rise above the race prejudices of his time, but was not able to comprehend the class and gender prejudices that suffused his work".

In the same number of the *Michigan Law Review* the editors published no fewer than six learned ripostes to Steven Lubet, of which three are worth mentioning here. Ann Althouse suggests that Atticus has good reason to believe Mayella is lying, if only because she refuses to answer further questions. William H. Simon suggests that unless Atticus thought Mayella was telling the truth, he would have had to test her story through a searching cross examination. It's true he humiliated the witness, but "in 1930s Alabama, an accusation of rape by a white woman against a black man was tantamount to a demand for the man's death". Randolph H. Stone supports Simon: "Mayella was not tortured (Emmett Till was tortured); she was simply cross-examined virgorously but with courtesy and respect, in contrast to the prosecution's racism-soaked cross-examination of Robinson."

The best of these extra-literary judgments of Atticus Finch came from Malcolm Gladwell, in a lively *New Yorker* article in 2009. He agrees with Lubet that in believing Tom Robinson and portraying Mayella and her father as white trash, Atticus is swapping one prejudice for another. His main critique of Harper Lee's hero, however, is that instead of being a racial reformer, he is a "Jim Crow liberal". In other words, he goes along with segregation for the time being, in the hope that racial justice will evolve through the gradual enlightenment of ordinary people's hearts and minds, rather than through changes in the law.

This notion that an iconic lawyer has little faith in the transforming force of legal judgments may sound odd, but the truth is that Atticus is no stickler for the law. Hearts and minds also govern in the case of Boo Radley after he has stabbed Tom Ewell in defense of the Finch children. To Sheriff Tate's suggestion that Ewell could be said to have fallen on his own knife Atticus reluctantly agrees. "Maybe you'll say it's my duty to tell the town all about it and not hush it up," says Tate to Atticus. "Know what'd happen then? All the ladies in

Maycomb includin' my wife'd be banging his door bringing angel food cakes. To my way of thinkin', Mr. Finch, taking the one man who's done you and this town a great service an' draggin' him with his shy ways into the limelight – to me, that's a sin." Like shooting a mockingbird, you might say. The great parental role model then passes the lesson on to his daughter: "'Scout,' he said, 'Mr. Ewell fell on his knife. Can you possibly understand?'" (30). But Malcolm Gladwell is having none of it:

Understand what? That her father and the sheriff have decided to obstruct justice in the name of saving their beloved neighbour the burden of angel-food cake? Atticus Finch is faced with jurors who have one set of standards for white people and another set for black folk like Tom Robinson. His response is to adopt one set of standards for respectable whites like Boo Radley and another for white trash like Bob Ewell. A book we thought instructed us about the world tells us, instead, about the limitations of Jim Crow liberalism in Maycomb, Alabama.

Eric Sundquist is right to claim that *To Kill a Mockingbird* displaces the contemporary crisis of the civil rights struggle in the "bygone era" of the Scottsboro trials and in the subplot of Boo Radley. It is also quite clear that these two diversions are not accidental, but part of a deliberate strategy on

Harper Lee's part. The central critical question is are they evasive or are they something else?

So much for the critique of Atticus as though a lawyer in real life. As one would expect, the analysis of the character in the novel includes his performance in court, but goes beyond it too. Probably the most weighty attack on Atticus within the context of Harper Lee's fictional strategy is that of Eric J. Sundquist's "Blues for Atticus Finch".

Sundquist starts with the old problem of the book's twin time frame. "The novel offers an anatomy of segregation at the moment of its legal destruction," he writes. But rather than confront the South's unjust and sometimes violent reaction to *Brown v. Board of Education*, "the novel harks back to the 1930s... to move the mounting fear and violence surrounding desegregation into an arena of safer contemplation, and to remind us, through a merciless string of moral lessons, that the children of Atticus Finch are the only hope for a future world of racial justice".

Another displacement, Lundquist suggests, is the subplot of Boo Radley, "a means to displace into more conventional gothic territory the Finch children's encounter with 'blackness'... Boo functions transparently as a harbinger of violated taboos and a displaced phantasm of racial fear, ultimately unmasked as the gentle, domesticated 'gray ghost' of harmonious integrations."

With all the "the book's dramatised racism and miscarriages of justice" thus safely displaced into a "bygone era", the character of Atticus Finch becomes "part of the novel's deceptive surface". On losing the court case, "Atticus suffers personal anguish and bitterness", but tells his children that bigoted juries and even lynch mobs are made up of people you know, and friends, who act reasonably in everyday life, and (as Lundquist paraphrases it) "that racial injustice is a southern problem that must be solved from within by right-thinking white people". Lundquist summarises the effect of Atticus's evasions as follows:

Whether to shield his children from the pain of racism or to shield Lee's southern readers from a confrontation with their own recalcitrance, Atticus, for all his devotion to the truth, sometimes lies. He employs indirection in order to teach his children about Maycomb's racial hysteria and the true meaning of courage, but he himself engages in evasion when he contends... that the Klu Klux Klan is a thing of the past... Indirection and displacement govern both the novel's pedagogy and, in the end, its moral stalemate.

And certainly Sundquist is right to complain – on purely literary-critical grounds, if none other – that we hear too much of "Atticus's voluble, nearly sacrosanct white voice", and not nearly enough of Tom Robinson's "proscribed, muted black voice".

To Kill a Mockingbird was written in the midst of one of the most radical shifts in political, social and cultural American history. It's worth remembering that the civil rights movement was set off by a ground-breaking legal judgment, and fought, piece by piece, by brave, intelligent, resourceful African Americans, whose voices – to go no further than the speeches of Martin Luther King Jr. – were neither "proscribed" nor "muted". So in the midst of this momentous historical process a novel that envisages the evolution of racial equality through the gradual enlightenment of individual conscience and the example set by right-thinking white men has some questions to answer.

The answer lies in those displacements noted by Lundquist. Take the first of these, the "bygone era" of the 1930s (and here we return to the narrower question of Atticus's skills as a lawyer). What none of the "real-life" school of legal analysts seems to have considered is that Atticus, despairing of the jury before whom Tom Robinson is to be tried, was working from the beginning to prepare the ground for an appeal. This is, after all, what he tells Jem the following morning: "It's not time to worry yet... There'll be an appeal, you can count on that" (22).

Nor is this just the consolation offered to a

small boy. The initial Scottsboro verdicts were repeatedly appealed – to the appellate court, the state supreme court, the federal supreme court (twice) – until by 1940 all but one of the defendants had either escaped or been paroled. In fact Gladwell cites the research of Lisa Lindquist Dorr to the effect that of 288 cases of black-on-white rape in Virginia between 1900 and 1960, 17 of the accused were lynched, 50 were executed, 48 given the maximum prison sentence, 52 sentenced to five years or less, 35 acquitted or had charges against them dropped, and "a not inconsiderable number had their sentenced commuted by the governor". Not an unmixedly glorious record, to be sure, but a far cry from William H. Simon's claim that in the South in the 1930s, "an accusation of rape by a white woman against a black man was tantamount to a demand for the man's death".

On what grounds could Atticus have appealed the Robinson verdict, had not Tom himself short-circuited the process by his suicidal attempt to escape? Well, apart from the jury disregarding the evidence teased out in Atticus's cross-examination of Bob and Mayella Ewell, there's the fact that the case went to court without medical evidence to support the charge in the first place. Even the first Scottsboro trial had that, and it was later used to discredit the chief witness for the prosecution. Then there was Mayella's refusal to answer further questions – "I got somethin' to say an' then I ain't gonna say no more" – on which Scout precociously comments: "I guess if she hadn't been so poor and ignorant, Judge Taylor would have put her under the jail for the contempt she had shown everybody in the court room" (18). Sadly, poverty and ignorance is no excuse. Mayella has indeed committed contempt of court, and the judge has overlooked it. This alone would be grounds for an appeal.

Finally, the Maycomb court, convened in the autumn of 1935, did not comply with *Norris v. Alabama*, decided on April 1 of that year. In this second major judgment to come out of the Scottsboro trials, the US Supreme Court decided that the exclusion of African Americans from a jury amounted to a violation of a defendant's constitutional right of due process. Were blacks excluded from the fictional Maycomb jury? They certainly were in real-life Alabama jurisdictions, like Jackson County and Morgan County, involved in the Scottsboro trials. Could Maycomb have found black jurors if it had wanted them? It's hard to see why people like the Rev. Sykes, or Calpurnia, who taught her son to read from Blackstone's *Commentaries*, could have been excluded on grounds other than colour.

Eric Sundquist is right to claim that *To Kill a Mockingbird* displaces Autherine Lucy, Rosa Parks, Emmett Till – and the whole crisis of the civil rights struggle contemporary to its composition and publication – in the "bygone era" of the Scottsboro trials and also in the subplot of Boo Radley. It is also quite clear that these two diversions are not accidental, but part of a deliberate strategy on Harper Lee's part. The central critical question is are they evasive or are they something else?

Let's take it step by step. To begin with, it's important to understand that the civil rights movement, and especially the southern white reaction to it, did not arise out of nowhere. *Brown v. Board of Education* re-awoke that fear – dormant, maybe, but still very powerful, potentially – of "intermarriage" between the sexes – in other words, interracial sexual relations, or miscegenation. Then the old black-on-white rape complex was reignited in the case of Emmett Till. Now suppose you are Harper Lee, wanting to deconstruct the contemporary phenomenon of the South's reaction to civil rights – that is, to re-imagine it in the context of its historical cultural, sociological, even psychological roots. You're no strenuous northern liberal, viewing the action from outside as a burning moral issue, but a southern girl, and a daughter of the white professional class – not black, not poor.

As they used to say in creative writing classes, you have to write what you know. You can't write from within the consciousness of the civil rights activist in the late 1950s, or of the African American at any time. You can't be Autherine Lucy or Rosa Parks any more than you can imagine what it's like to inhabit Tom Robinson's mind and family.

So assume you want to write about the contemporary South, including the civil rights movement, but need to limit your story to what you know, writing to and for your southern neighbours. How would you start? With the family dynamics of a lawyer's household, since your father was a lawyer; with the law itself, since you studied the subject at university. Then, since you want (as Harper Lee said she did) to be the Jane Austen of South Alabama, you might be drawn to a satirical view of the local polite white society. That portrait you might hope to extend into a more ambitious fictional recreation of a southern town – its history, its traditional culture, its prejudices, superstitions and fears.

The big question is could these essentially local topics, imagined as happening 20 years before, become the fictional analogues of the civil rights struggle, removed in time from the present but connected as they are by the same motivators, the same private and public psychology in the same social space?

At first sight the Boo Radley subplot could not seem more remote from the civil rights movement. Indeed, as Sundquist says, it is "a means to displace into more conventional gothic territory the Finch's children's encounter with 'blackness'". Introduced to the reader as a "malevolent phantom", Boo is the object of superstition on the part of both black and white residents of Maycomb. African Americans whistle and cross the street to pass his house. White children won't touch the pecans that fall from his trees into the schoolyard. Baseballs hit in error on to the Radley land go unfetched. He is believed to go out at night to spy into people's windows, even to mutilate chickens and household pets.

Yet Scout Finch's curiosity about Boo develops into genuine empathy. That plus Boo's defence of the children serves to demystify him, to unmask him, as Sundquist puts it, "as the gentle, domesticated 'grey ghost' of harmonious integration":

> The novel's concluding Halloween sequence… tells us the true danger comes from "white trash" ("Boo" evolves into the insidious "Bob"); and it offers the illusion that racial hysteria – the Klan, night-riding mobs, the White Citizens Council – can be likewise unmasked, humiliated, and brought to justice once the South disposes of its childish fears and moves forward into a post-*Brown* world.

This is very acute. That's exactly how the "Boo" subplot works: as a way of showing that racial panics, after all, were no more substantial than the fear of ghosts, and other things you say "Boo" to. But why Sundquist's use of the word "illusion"? Didn't the South really dispose of its childish fears and move forward into a post-*Brown* world? Wasn't that exactly what happened?

With the old trial in a "bygone era", Sundquist's same critique of evasion can also be turned into critical praise. The conservatism of Harper Lee's novel, he writes, lies in "its palpable attempt both to register the reappearance of the South's rape complex in the Till case and to displace it into the time past of Scottsboro, to fold it into the South's narrative but at the same time banish it to a nightmare from which the South might yet awake". Exactly so. The trial of Tom Robinson evokes the Scottsboro trials, both to provide an analogue for the violence, injustice and fear of racial mixing highlighted by the Till trial (and the myriad other reactions to Brown) and to suggest that one day even these latter events may come to seem an old nightmare. And isn't that what happened? Hasn't the American South awakened indeed from its old nightmare?

It comes as a shock to recall that over half a century has now elapsed since *To Kill a Mockingbird* was published – more than twice as long as the time gap between the novel's setting and date of composition. For that matter, it's been 17 years since Sundquist published his critique of the novel's displacements, with the result that his strictures about awakening from old nightmares have begun to look more literal and accurate than illusory.

That is not to say that any of this could have happened without Brown, the white South's reaction to that radical and authoritative judgment and the African-American determination to make a reality of Martin Luther Jr.'s dream that "one day right there in Alabama little black boys and black girls will be able to join hands with little white boys and white girls as sisters and brothers". Atticus is wrong to imply that a gradual evolution in the white southern conscience could put an end to segregation.

But then, despite the assumption underlying the Michigan Law Review discussion, Atticus was not a real lawyer but a character in a novel, in ironic juxtaposition to forces generated by the immediate fictional plot and the more distant plot of southern obsessions, both past and contemporary. Navigating between Atticus's voluble moral lessons and the realities "out there", those displacements into the legal past and into the gothic fantasies surrounding Boo Radley are a way by indirection to find direction out. As part of a documentary account of the end of segregation these displacements would be a way of dodging the subject. As they work in the fiction of *To Kill a Mockingbird* they are more prescient than evasive.

How does the book relate to the stereotypes of southern fiction?

To Kill a Mockingbird stands in a complex relationship to the conventions of American southern fiction. Understanding how Harper Lee addresses and debates with her literary models provides important insights into what she is up to in the novel.

Before the Civil War two of the more prominent southern novelists were John Pendleton Kennedy and William Gilmore Simms. Kennedy produced sentimental sketches of plantation life, like *Swallow Barn* (1832), while Simms, a disciple of Walter Scott, was more given to frontier adventures, as in *The Yemassee* (1835), where Native Americans stood in for Scott's Highlanders. Both were avid supporters of slavery and the plantation economy. Simms even wrote an attack on Harriet Beecher Stowe's *Uncle Tom's Cabin*, called *The Sword and the Distaff* (1852). Following the South's defeat in the Civil War the dominant theme in popular fiction of the region was the lost cause of the Confederacy. Leading the new fashion was Thomas Nelson Page, whose novels idealised life before the Civil War, when slaves were contented and their masters high-minded, idealistic patriarchs.

Part of the "lost cause" mood was bitterness about Reconstruction, the harsh peace imposed on the South, when the victorious North used the army to impose desegregated civil government, gave the vote to the freed slaves and founded state schools for everyone. The most outspoken fictional reaction to this unwelcome revolution was the "Reconstruction Trilogy" by Thomas Dixon, Jr., of which *The Clansman* (1906) provided the story for D. W. Griffiths's landmark film *The Birth of a Nation* (1915), in which the Ku Klux Klan rode in as heroic defenders against the exploitative "carpetbaggers" from the North and the southern "scalawags" who sold out to them, and stood sturdily as the barrier between the freed blacks and the voting booth.

Undoubtedly the most popular of the lost-cause novels was Margaret Mitchell's *Gone with the Wind* (1936), and especially the movie made of the book, released in 1940. Mitchell repeated the motifs of happy plantation life destroyed by cataclysmic invasion, post-war anarchy of scalawags, ex-slaves, both loyal and uppity, and the avenging Klan. The title alone proclaimed the lost culture and society of the southern plantation. Stereotypes arising from this literature include the cult of the southern gentleman, along with various caricatures of African Americans and poor white trash. All three are important for understanding how *To Kill a Mockingbird* works.

The first of these, according to Claudia Durst Johnson, "was an image of a gallant, romantic gentleman who, like the landed gentry of England, loved high adventure, had impeccable manners... a man of action with an exaggerated sense of chivalry". The best example is Ashley Wilkes, with whom Scarlett O'Hara, tempestuous heroine of *Gone with the Wind*, is perpetually in love, even though (or possibly because) she doesn't understand him.

Johnson offers a typical early example of the stereotype, in the form of General McDowell Keith, "a gentleman of the old kind" in Thomas Nelson Page's *Gordon Keith* (1903). At the start of the Civil War Gordon is "sent for to come home". The next morning he comes downstairs to find his father, the old gent

> standing in the drawing room dressed in full uniform... the resemblance to the man-in-armor in the picture over the library mantel suddenly struck the boy. There was the high look, the same light in the eyes, the same gravity about the mouth; and when his father, after taking leave of the servants, rode away in his gray uniform, on the bay horse "Chevalier," with his sword by his side... and let Gordon accompany him for the first few miles, the boy felt as though he had suddenly been transported to a world of which he had read, and were riding behind a knight of old. Ah! If only there

were a few Roundheads formed at the gate, how they would scatter them!

Atticus Finch couldn't be further from this ideal. Take his name, for a start. A number of figures in the classical world took the sobriquet "Atticus" (the Roman word for the area around Athens), but the most likely source of the name Harper Lee chose for Scout's father is Titus Pomponius Atticus, aristocratic scholar, author, patron of the arts and close friend of Cicero. Whereas General Keith cannot wait to dress up for the American Civil War, Titus Pomponius Atticus moved to Athens to avoid taking sides in the civil war between Sulla and Cinna.

Atticus Finch is half blind. Secretly he plays the jew's harp, to Scout's disgust when Miss Maudie tells her so (10). He doesn't hunt or fish or play poker, smoke or drink along with the other fathers. He won't teach Jem and Scout to shoot their air rifles , allowing them to get on with the pastime on their own, while warning them not to shoot mockingbirds.

Yet when there's a rabid dog to be put out of its misery, only Atticus can be trusted to do it. Not even Sheriff Tate can risk shooting, missing and further enraging the dog so that it becomes a general menace to the community. Atticus bags the animal with one shot, despite stepping on his own glasses:

*"Well now, Miss Jean Louise," [Maudie] said,
"still think your father can't do anything?"*

"Nome," I said meekly.

*"Forgot to tell you the other day that besides
playing the jew's harp, Atticus Finch was the
deadliest shot in Maycomb County in his time."*

(10)

Black literary stereotypes were founded on a
contradictory mixture of exotic fascination with
the Other, and a condescending view of the
familiar African American, best exemplified by
their treatment in *Gone with the Wind* and Ulrich
B. Phillips's standard history, *American Negro
Slavery* (1918), in which the institution was
explained in terms of the African-American's
genetic and cultural backwardness.

Other popular sources include the vaudeville
stage, blackface minstrel shows and the movies.
There were four stock figures: the Tom, the zip
coon, the buck and the mammy. Toms were
compliant and long suffering, religious and loyal to
their masters, no matter how badly treated. Bucks
were sullen, often violent and forever after white
women. The zip coon, according to Donald Bogle,
was a satire on freed blacks, "good for nothing
more than eating watermelons, stealing chickens,
shooting craps, or butchering the English
language". Mammies were household slaves, "big,
fat and cantankerous", though capable of kindness

and good temper.

Toms go back to *Uncle Tom's Cabin* (1852) by Harriet Beecher Stowe, in which the Tom of the title is sold down the river, eventually winding up as slave to the sadistic Simon Legree, who beats him when he refuses to stop reading the Bible and finally orders his overseer to kill him when he refuses to inform on an escaped slave.

As a lost-cause novel, *Gone with the Wind* promotes the old confederacy line that slaves loved their masters. The naïve and trusting Big Sam even digs trenches to help the white folks hide in when the marauding Union soldiers start to move on to the plantations. When the South falls and the slaves are freed, not one of them wants to leave Tara, Scarlett's plantation.

Because they were so reassuring to a white market, Toms had their commercial application too. The genial figure of Uncle Ben, the elderly black man in a bow tie, was the smiling face on the box of the famous "converted" – that is, parboiled – rice. His picture is supposed to be that of Frank Brown, the *maître de* of a Chicago restaurant favoured by the firm's executives.

How does this bear on *To Kill a Mockingbird*? There are no zip coons in the story, and no bucks either, though in the trial prosecuting attorney Horace Gilmer taunts Tom with the term when he asks: "'Were you so scared that she'd hurt you, you ran, a big buck like you?'". But is Tom himself a stereotyped Uncle Tom? He is certainly long-suffering enough, and sorely tempted by being falsely accused and his life put in jeopardy, but he lacks the self-sacrificing patience of the original Tom. He panics and bolts, forcing the guards to shoot him down as he tries to escape. Moreover, on the witness stand he sounds more like the Scottsboro boys than he does Uncle Tom. The truth is, though Tom Robinson is not fully fledged as a character, he is no stereotype either.

What about the Mammy figure? Again, the first fully formed mammy comes from *Uncle Tom's Cabin.* (It's ironic that the two most iconic stereotypes in southern fiction should have come out of that anti-slavery novel.) Stowe's description of Aunt Chloe set the visual framework for thousands of mammies to come:

> *A round, black, shiny face is hers, so glossy as to suggest the idea that she might have been washed over by the whites of eggs, like one of her own tea rusks. Her whole plump countenance beams with satisfaction and contentment from under a well-starched checkered turban bearing on it.*

Like all caricatures, writes David Pilgrim, that of the mammy contained a little truth surrounded by a larger lie. The caricature portrayed an obese, coarse, maternal figure. She had great love for her white "family", but often treated her own family with disdain. Although she had children, sometimes many, she was completely desexualised. She "belonged" to the white family. She had no black friends; the white family was her entire world.

Mammies were a crucial part of the plantation propaganda, physically emblematic of the bounty of the planter's household, while looking sufficiently fat and ugly to counteract abolitionists' rumours of miscegenation. They infiltrated popular fiction too, as well as entertainments like vaudeville, minstrel shows, the movies, even television. The mammy in *The Birth of a Nation* defends her old master's home against marauding soldiers. In *The Jazz Singer* (1927), the first sound movie, Al Jolson in blackface sings "I'd walk a million miles for one of your smiles" to his Mammy back in old Alabamee.

As with Atticus and the southern gentleman, Harper Lee could not have overturned the mammy stereotype more deliberately. Far from being plump and rounded, Calpurnia is "all angles and bones". In the absence of their mother she is virtually a foster mother to Jem and Scout. She takes practical charge of their behaviour, and "Atticus always took her side" (12).

Where Calpurnia really departs from the traditional mammy in fiction, commerce and popular entertainment, though, is in having a life, family and friends of her own. Granted, Carson McCullers did something of the sort with Berenice Brown in *The Member of the Wedding*. Like Calpurnia, Berenice is something of a foster mother to Frankie Addams and even John Henry West, whom she tells stories of her life with past husbands.

But whereas the children get to *hear* something of Berenice's past life outside the family, Scout and Jem are invited to *walk into* Calpurnia's present, when they accompany her to Sunday service at the First Purchase African M. E. Church. There the children are met with some hostility, but much more cordiality.

They discover that Calpurnia speaks to her friends in an accent different from the one she uses in the Finch household. They meet the Reverend Sykes and Lula. They meet Zeebo, Calpurnia's eldest son, now grown up with a family of his own, and whom – far from ignoring – Calpurnia has taught to read from the Bible and Blackstone's *Commentaries*. He is the church's music superintendent because he can line out the hymns – that is, read them out, line by line – for the rest of the congregation to follow. They learn of Helen Robinson's predicament now that Tom is in prison and not earning – one of the few insights the reader gets of Tom's family life – and they discover how genially, though relentlessly, the Reverend Sykes extracts enforced charity in action through the collection for her support.

All this comes as a surprise to Scout:

*That Calpurnia had a modest double life never
dawned on me. The idea that she had a separate
existence outside our household was a novel one,
to say nothing of her having command of two
languages. (12)*

Indeed, it's part of Scout's learning trajectory that
is the book's plot, and one of the most important
lessons she learns.

So much for the African-American stereotypes.
What about the other end of the white social scale,
the figure of "white trash"? The term started out as
a black response to insults like "Nigger," but it was
quickly adopted in white usage too, as a way of
discriminating between the deserving and
undeserving poor – a distinction that persists in *To
Kill a Mockingbird* too. In his memoir of growing
up in the South, Vernon Johnson recalls the two
kinds of poor white, as seen from his family's
perspective. "The poor people we knew," he writes,
"were very much like us":

They were devout church-goers and devoted family
members. Most were intelligent and believed in
working hard, living upright lives and keeping
meticulously clean, even if their clothes were made
of flour sacks.

Yet there were others, whom they didn't know and who were not "like us". They were uneducated and "totally ignorant even of the world around them, dirty, diseased, immoral, destitute".

Disease, dirt, immorality, degeneracy: this is what set white trash off from the respectable poor. The writer Virginia Poster Durr recalls seeing the white trash troop past their house on Saturday mornings, on their way into Birmingham, Alabama: "miserable looking, pale and stunted and almost deformed". But then, as her family reassured her, their condition was just a force of nature:

> I was told by my mother and father and everyone whom I respected and loved that these people were just that way. They were just poor white trash. If they had pellagra and worms and malaria and if they were thin and hungry and immoral, it was just because that was the way they were. It was in their blood. They were born to be poor white trash.

As in personal recollections of the South, so the white trash figure looms in popular southern fiction. After a particularly fraught scene with Ashley Wilkes, when he blurts out that he loves her, but (yet again) steadfastly refuses to leave Melanie, Scarlett O'Hara scoops up a handful of Tara's red soil and kneads it into a ball. "'Yes,' she said, 'I've still got this.'" Just then a carriage drives up to the front steps of Tara, and the driver steps down to help his lady passenger alight. He is Jonas Wilkerson, their former overseer, now newly enriched by a job with the Freedman's Bureau and illegal deals in cotton.

He has come to make Scarlett a (low) offer on her house and estate. But it's the woman who catches her attention:

> Scarlett saw at a glance that the dress was bright in color to the point of vulgarity...
> "Why, it's Emmie Slattery!" she cried, so surprised she spoke the world aloud.
> "Yes'm, it's me," said Emmie, tossing her head with an ingratiating smile and starting toward the steps.
> Emmie Slattery! The dirty, tow-headed slut whose illegitimate baby Ellen had baptized, Emmie who had given typhoid to Ellen and killed her. This overdressed, common, nasty piece of poor white trash was coming up the steps of Tara, bridling and grinning as if she belonged here...
> "Get off those steps, you trashy wench!" she cried. "Get off this land! Get out!"

Here "white trash" is partly a term of class abuse (that vulgar colour), but the image retains the strains of disease and low morals. Even Emmie's surname suggests "slattern," a word for a dirty woman, a slut, even a prostitute.

Almost contemporary with *Gone with the Wind*, the fiction of Erskine Caldwell was positively rolling – not to say revelling – in white trash. Jeeter Lester in *Tobacco Road* (1932), whose "feeblemindness" is inherited, has sired 17 children, of whom 12 are still living. While the Lesters fight over a sack of turnips, Jeeter's hare-lipped daughter Ellie May fornicates with her sister's husband in a dirt road. In *God's Little Acre* (1933), Ty Ty Walden commiserates with one of his sons over his "diseased" wife, while another son sleeps with two of his sisters-in-law in turn, and "Darling Jill" fornicates with an Albino in full view of her family.

Surprisingly, the stereotype of poor white trash goes wholly unchallenged in *To Kill a Mockingbird*. Even the strenuously tolerant Atticus, who teaches his daughter that the word "nigger" is "common" (9), and who refuses to hate even Hitler, considers the Ewells to be "absolute trash" – or at least that's what Scout reports him as saying. And even she notices the disparity from his usual equanimity, as she tells Calpurnia: "I never heard Atticus talk about folks the way he talked about the Ewells" (12).

So Malcom Gladwell is right to say that in defending Tom Robinson Atticus interrogates Bob and Mayella Ewell is such a way as to encourage the jury to swap one prejudice for another, hoping that their class-based contempt for the white trash will trump their racism.

Does he do this for tactical reasons, to beat a tough rap? Not entirely; as Scout has noticed with surprise, his dislike of white trash is one prejudice Atticus holds with conviction, outside as well as inside the courthouse. And at the beginning of the trial, even before Atticus has begun his cross questioning of Bob and Mayella Ewell, that suspicion has infiltrated the novel's prose:

> Every town the size of Maycomb had families like the Ewells... No truant officers could keep their numerous offspring in school; no public health officer could keep them free from congenital defects, various worms, and the diseases indigenous to filthy surroundings.

The Ewells live "behind the garbage dump" in a "cabin" resting "uneasily upon four irregular lumps of limestone", its windows "merely open spaces in the walls, which in the summer times were covered with greasy strips of cheese-cloth to keep out the varmints that feasted on Maycomb's refuse" (17). This is Scout speaking, in her retrospective adult's voice, so whether or not she thought it at the time, she certainly did while telling the story. It comes over as the town consensus as well as the authorial view.

It's all reminiscent of the notorious *Hollow Folk*

(1933), that supposedly scientific study of the country poor living in the Blue Ridge Mountains in western Virginia, but which was covert propaganda for removing the hillbillies to make way for the Shenandoah National Park in the mid 1930s.

Of the five communities studied in *Hollow Folk*, culturally the most backward was called "Colvin Hollow" (actually Corbin Hollow, Madison Country, Virginia). Although it was less than 100 miles from the nation's capital in Washington, it had no community government, no organised religion, little social organisation wider than that of the family and clan, and only traces of organised industry. The ragged children, until 1928, had never seen the flag or heard of the Lord's Prayer.

> A new-born baby lies with its parents – and perhaps one or two other children – on a sack of cornhusks covered with rags... The strong scent of urine rises from the bedding, and mingles with other body smells and the odors of cooking... During the warm days of spring hosts of flies fresh from their feasts on human excrement deposited in the woods, pour into the cabin and settle on the infant.

Housing was primitive, consisting of "log cabins, of which only a very few had front porches and one glass window nailed in place". The similarity to the Ewells' way of the life is obvious: the "home" as a cabin, the proximity to human waste infecting the vulnerable, the remoteness from social and civil institutions, the numberless children.

The last southern literary stereotype to be considered, the southern gothic, is not a matter of content, but of style and genre. The fashion for so-called "gothic" romance – that is fiction set vaguely in a version of the late medieval era – flourished in England and Germany in the late 18th century. Typically, settings were in mysterious castles with hundreds of secret passages and dark alleyways, situated in the Alps or Apennines, or other exotic locations seldom seen by their readers. Plots often involved innocent maidens being held captive by scheming tyrants – as often for their money as their bodies. Because it frequently purported to be an ancient tale found in an old manuscript, gothic romance could slip the bounds of fictional realism. Dialogue was stylised or otherwise high-flown; plots moved as often to supernatural as to naturalistic stimuli.

The gothic style crossed the Atlantic to pop up in the fiction of Charles Brockden Brown. His titles alone give an idea of his fictional mode – *Wieland; or, the Transformation* (1798), *Edgar Huntley; or, Memories of a Sleep-Walker* (1799). His plots were sensational, often violent, and hinged, if not on the supernatural, then certainly on mystery and unlikely coincidences.

But it was in the American South that the gothic really flourished. The list of southern gothic writers is long, distinguished and surprisingly recent, including novels by Carson McCullers, Eudora Welty, Flannery O'Connor and James Dickey, the plays of Tennessee Williams, and above all the vast fictional project of William Faulkner.

The gothic gravitated to the American South particularly because the region provided so many plausible stage sets suggesting a past of melodramatic adventures – decaying mansions in grounds dripping with Spanish moss – and a history of exotic social and racial hierarchies no longer current in the modern United States. Compared to its European model, the southern gothic wasn't much involved with the supernatural. The mystery that took its place was – in Faulkner's case, especially – the irretrievability of the past, as family sagas worked their way down through the history of the South. *Absalom, Absalom* (1936) traces the rise and fall of the family patriarch Thomas Sutpen, as he tries to build, then struggles to keep, and finally loses a dynastic estate, through four generations of miscegenation, incest and violence.

Sutpen's unstable mental state is another feature typical of southern gothic novels. Quentin Compson in *The Sound and the Fury* (1929) is obsessed with his sister Caddie's sexuality, and the distress eventually drives him to suicide. On the stage, Blanche DuBois in Tennessee Williams's *A Streetcar Named Desire* (1947) is a faded, delusional southern belle living in the past, yet with plenty of flirtatious moves left. Carson McCullers's eccentric protagonists suffer bewildering varieties of loneliness. And so on.

Harper Lee is often classified as a southern gothic writer. To see just how wrong this is, you have only to compare *To Kill a Mockingbird* with the first published novel by Harper Lee's childhood friend, Truman Capote, on whom she based the character Dill. Capote wrote most of *Other Voices, Other Rooms* (1948) in Monroeville, Alabama, the source for Lee's Maycomb, yet the novel's setting is not the town but a decaying mansion on an isolated plantation outside it. Joel, an effeminate boy, abandoned by his mother, is sent to live with his father, his depressive step-mother Amy and Randolph, a debauched transvestite. Randolph wears things like "a seersucker Kimono with butterfly sleeves" over his pyjamas, and on "his plumpish feet" a "pair of tooled leather sandals" showing his toenails polished to a "manicured gloss". By contrast, such references to clothing as we get in *To Kill a Mockingbird* are to plain overalls – except, significantly, for Dill's blue linen shorts that buttoned to his shirt.

Other descriptions in Harper Lee's novel concentrate on sights open to the public gaze: streets, the town square, the outsides of houses. Even the inside of the courthouse is a public space. In *Other Voices, Other Rooms*, though, the focus is on interiors, often hidden – even secret and mysterious – as in this description of the ground floor of the decaying mansion:

> The parlour of Scully's Landing ran the ground-floor's length; gold draperies tied with satin tassels obscured the greater part of its dusky, deserted interior... a gilded love-seat of lilac velvet, an Empire sofa next to a marble fireplace, and a cabinet, one of three, the others which were indistinct, gleaming with china figurines and ivory fans and curios... a Japanese pagoda, an ornate shepherd lamp, chandelier prisms dangling from its geranium globe like jewelled icicles.

The plot of *Other Voices, Other Rooms* is similarly exotic. Though this isn't the place to tell the story at length, suffice it to say that Joel's father is mysteriously absent until he is finally revealed to the boy as a mute quadriplegic, a condition caused by his falling down stairs after being accidentally shot by Randolph. About the only note of relative normality is Idabel, a tomboy clearly based – again significantly – on Harper Lee, but bigger, faster, noisier and more outspoken than Scout Finch, whom Joel befriends as an escape from the hothouse of Scully's Landing.

Now *that's* gothic. By contrast, because it demystifies so many stereotypes of southern fiction, *To Kill a Mockingbird* might more accurately be called an anti-gothic novel. As we have already seen, the Boo Radley subplot is deliberately invoked as a southern-gothic mystery of hidden supernatural horrors, only to be uncovered as a realistic interaction between people whose motives are entirely explicable in the real world. To a lesser extent the novel also deconstructs topics involved in the complex fate of southern history, from the region's racism to the lost cause of the Confederacy.

The crucial clue to understanding Harper Lee's relationship to the southern gothic style lies in her admiration for Jane Austen. "All I want to be is the Jane Austen of south Alabama," she told Roy Newquist in March 1964. In this possibly self-mocking comment she was nevertheless seriously proclaiming a realistic style, an interest in the local and the portrayal of social interaction – in other words, novelistic concerns wholly opposed to the gothic romance.

It's worth remembering that, in 1798-99, Jane Austen herself wrote the first ever anti-gothic novel, *Northanger Abbey*, in which she also, as it happens, created perhaps the first tomboy in English fiction. Now the English gothic novels of the late 18th century typically demystified themselves in the course of their dénouements, since in an era already well advanced in scientific discovery reason had largely discredited the supernatural. So in Mrs Radcliffe's *The Mysteries of Udolpho* (1794) the ghosts that the orphaned heroine Emily hears and sees are really pirates hiding in the castle, entering and leaving through a secret passageway, and a horrific figure behind a veil turns out to be a wax dummy.

In explaining their supernatural turns in the light of reason, Radcliffe and the other gothic romancers were treating their readers to an entertaining intellectual exercise, on the level of solving a puzzle or resolving a detective story. Jane Austen's manoeuvre was much more radical. It was to turn the melodramatic into the moral – or, to put it another way, to reinvent the romance as a novel.

Catherine Morland, who has grown up as a tomboy but is now on the marriage market, is invited to visit her new acquaintances, Eleanor and Henry Tilney, at their family seat, Northanger Abbey. As a great fan of gothic romances, Catherine expects the old country house to be full of dark corridors and secret passages, and she is not disappointed when she finds out that a set of rooms, always kept locked, had been the quarters of her friends' deceased mother. Gradually she comes to suspect their father, General Tilney, of having imprisoned his wife, in true gothic fashion, or even of murdering her.

When Catherine finally gains entry to the rooms, she finds out that there is nothing suspicious about them at all, and she is devastated when Henry, with whom she has fallen in love, rebukes her for her fantasies.

They make it up, and the young people spend several happy days together when the General goes off to London. But suddenly he returns in a terrible temper, and Catherine is, suddenly and inexplicably, evicted from the house. It is only later, when Henry visits her at her home, that she learns the General turned violently against her when he discovered that her family was too poor to make her a suitable match for his son.

So Catherine learns two things: that the old country house has no guilty secrets, no fanciful mysteries in the gothic sense; and that the real horrors emanate from the vile snobbery of the present owner. This is a lesson in aesthetics too. For it is the novel, as opposed to the romance (gothic or otherwise), that is "the most effective agent of the moral imagination", as Lionel Trilling has put it, that involves "the reader himself in the moral life, inviting him to put his own motives under examination", teaching "the extent of human variety and the value of this variety". This is the measure of *To Kill a Mockingbird* too: that it dispenses with the dusty old machinery of ghosts, spooks and superstition in favour of the wider humanity of choice, replaces magic with morals.

Has *To Kill a Mockingbird* outlived its time?

Introducing his useful collection of essays on the novel, Yale professor Harold Bloom admits that Scout Finch "seems to me better than her book, which has dated into a period piece, while she herself remains remarkably vital and refreshing". By "period piece" he meant "outdated", not the more neutral "set in a particular period". But outdated in what respect? In its form as an old-fashioned realistic novel? In its coverage of a "race problem" now much moved on? In its judgements, as voiced by Atticus?

The 50th anniversary of the novel's appearance prompted a good deal of revisionary comment. As Scott Herring paraphrases the mood in a lively piece in *The New English* Review: "While the novel retains its sentimental, tear-jerking charms, it has lost the status it once held as a bold indictment of racism, and today is more likely to be condemned for not indicting racism boldly enough."

Central to this feeling that the book's social edge has got a bit blunt over time is a certain weariness with Atticus Finch's pronouncements. Writing in *The Wall Street Journal* of June 24, 2010, Allen Barra calls Atticus a "repository of cracker-barrel epigrams", who "speaks in snatches of dialogue that seem written to be quoted in high-school English papers". Pauline Kael, film critic of *The New Yorker*, called Gregory Peck as Atticus "virtuously dull", and chided the movie for its tone of "Hollywood self-congratulation for its enlightened racial attitudes".

Yet people should be careful of imposing today's values on yesterday's fiction. Racial attitudes in the South have come a long way since the late 1950s – not to mention the early 1930s, when *To Kill a Mockingbird* is set. Another important reminder is that Atticus Finch is a character in a novel, not a real person. In its concentration on the trial and its centring of Atticus as an almost prophetic figure, the movie must bear some of the blame for this complex of errors.

In stripping the action down largely to the trial, the film cuts out or marginalises other agents of the children's development. "Unfortunately, the figure of Atticus Finch sucks up all the oxygen," as Herring has put it, "especially as given to us by Gregory Peck, lumbering around like a statue come to life." Crucial events and dialogues involving Calpurnia, Maudie and above all Mrs Dubose shrink or disappear in the movie, and along with them, the complex strands in the children's education. If the book consisted solely of Tom's trial and the events surrounding it, it would be about race. As it is, it is about three children who start out in mischief and make-believe, then gradually mature into the recognition and acceptance of moral ambiguity.

The racial issues raised by Tom's indictment and trial are part of that development. So also are Maudie's lesson about Atticus's marksmanship, Mrs Dubose's abusive dependence on Jem, Aunt Alexandra's strictures on Scout's dress code and her reiteration of the Finch family background, the quiet example that Boo Radley sets Scout and Jem in unobtrusive charity, and dozens of other encounters. It's true that Atticus mediates some of these lessons – about Mrs Dubose, for example – but in others he has no part. They are prompted

WHY DID HARPER LEE WRITE ONLY ONE NOVEL?

Rumours abound. The most outlandish is that her childhood friend Truman Capote really wrote *To Kill a Mockingbird*, and wasn't around in her life to repeat the favour. Anyone who has read his own novel set in Monroeville, Alabama, will realise that Capote could never have adjusted his prose style, his interests or his early fondness for the gothic mode to suit Lee's interests.

Did fame come too quickly, too overwhelmingly? American literature has provided other sad examples of one-trick ponies come to grief. Ross Lockridge's *Raintree County* and Thomas Heggen's *Mister Roberts*, both published in 1946, were bestsellers rapidly given major theatrical treatments – the first in a 1957 MGM by Calpurnia, or Maudie, or just intuited by the children themselves following striking experiences.

Some of Atticus's maxims, like his stress on tolerance, are indeed dull, but no less crucial to the children's education for that. Others are fatuous, like his claim (in the 1930s!) that the Ku Klux Klan has dwindled to little more than a benevolent society, like the Elks – a lie told, no doubt, to quieten his children's fears.

If we were to take all Atticus's maxims as authorial – that is, exactly what the author thinks and wants her readers to think – then we would

movie starring a whole constellation of Hollywood stars, including Elizabeth Taylor, Montgomery Clift and Eva Marie Saint, and the second in a smash-hit Broadway play, followed by a Warner Brothers film in 1955, with Henry Fonda playing the title role in both.

In both cases the novelists' vocation failed to survive their success. Despite, or maybe because of intense pressure from agents and publishers to produce further work, they couldn't face scaling the cliff of their fame to write further. Both became blocked, and by the end of the decade both had committed suicide.

Harper Lee may also have suffered writers' block after *To Kill a Mockingbird*. Asked by Roy Newquist in March, 1964, if she was now working on another novel, she answered, "Yes, and it goes slowly, ever so slowly." Apparently it was to have been another story set in a small Alabama town, and was to be called "The Long Goodbye".

But whereas Lockridge and Heggen had been dazzled by their success, indeed have at least two grounds for critical complaint: that the judgements themselves are banal, and the novel flawed in showing one thing, that life is more complicated than we thought, while telling the opposite, that Dad can lay down the law to settle all issues. Instead Atticus's pronouncements are limited to their time and place, and no doubt some are simplified as answers to an eagerly inquiring daughter. Atticus is a character like anyone else in the novel, fixed by his class, his gradualist political convictions, by what he sees as his responsibilities as a citizen, a lawyer, a legislator, and above all a parent.

sudden fame came to Harper Lee as a less welcome experience. "It was like being hit over the head and knocked cold," she told Newquist. "I was hoping for a quick and merciful death at the hands of the reviewers … and in some ways this [celebrity] was just about as frightening as the quick, merciful death I'd expected." So even if she could repeat the triumph, would she have welcomed it?

Besides, she had a community to go home to, one of people who knew her and her family, and who would always accept her, with or without a world-wide reputation. Even at the height of her literary prominence, she lived only two months out of the year in New York. "I enjoy New York," she told Newquist, "theatres. movies, concerts, all that – and I have many friends here. But I always go home again."

She still lives in Monroeville, where her friends and neighbours see her regularly, while still guarding her privacy ∎

A SHORT CHRONOLOGY

1852 Harriet Beecher Stowe's *Uncle Tom's Cabin*

1861-65 American Civil War

1884 Mark Twain's *Adventures of Huckleberry Finn*

1926 April 28 Nelle Harper Lee born in Monroeville, Alabama, the youngest of four children of Amasa Coleman Lee and Frances Cunningham Finch.

1931-37 The Scottsboro rape trials

1932 Harper Lee befriends Truman Capote, who had been sent to live with relatives in Monroeville.

1933-35 Years in which *To Kill a Mockingbird* is set

1936 Margaret Mitchell's *Gone With The Wind*

1944 Harper Lee starts at Huntingdon, a women's college in Alabama. In 1945 she transfers to the University of Alabama to study law. In 1949 she leaves law school for New York to pursue her writing, working at the reservations desks of Eastern Air Lines and British Overseas Airways Corporation.

1946 Carson McCullers's *The Member of the Wedding*, an important source for *Mockingbird*

1948 Truman Capote bases the character Isabel in *Other Voices, Other Rooms* on Harper Lee.

1954 US Supreme Court rules on *Brown vs. Board of Education.*

1955-56 Arrest of Rosa Parks; Montgomery Bus Boycott in Alabama

1956 December **Having found an agent,** Harper Lee is given a year's wages by friends to enable her to concentrate on her writing.

1957 Congress passes the Civil Rights Act following the outcry after the murder of Emmett Till.

1959 Harper Lee travels with Truman Capote to Kansas to help him research for *In Cold Blood,* published in 1966.

1960 July 11 *To Kill a Mockingbird* published

1962 December 25 Film of *To Kill a Mockingbird*

1964 Congress passes another Civil Rights Act which bans discrimination based on "race, color, religion, or national origin" in employment practices and public accommodation.

2008 November 5 President George W. Bush presents Harper Lee with the Presidential Medal of Freedom, explaining "at a critical moment in our history, her beautiful book, *To Kill a Mockingbird,* helped focus the nation on the turbulent struggle for equality".

BIBLIOGRAPHY

Barra, Allen, "What 'To Kill a Mockingbird' Isn't", *The Wall Street Journal*, June 24, 2010.

Bloom, Harold, ed., *Harper Lee's To Kill a Mockingbird. Bloom's Modern Critical Interpretations*, updated edition, New York: Chelsea House, 2007.

Bogle, Donald, *Toms, Coons, Mulattoes, Mammies and Bucks: An Interpretive History of Blacks in American Films*. New York: Continuum, 1973; part reprinted in Claudia Johnson, (q.v.), 175-177.

Chura, Patrick, "Prolepsis and Anachronism: Emmett Till and the Historicity of To Kill a Mockingbird", *Southern Literary Journal*, vol. 32 (2000); reprinted in Bloom (q.v.), 115-140.

Durr, Virginia Foster, *Outside the Magic Circle: The Autobiography of Virginia Foster Durr*. Tuscaloosa: the University of Alabama Press, 1985; selection in Claudia Johnson, (q.v.), 85.

Fiedler, Leslie, *Love and Death in the American Novel*, Penguin, 1960

Gladwell, Malcolm, "The Courthouse Ring: Atticus Finch and the Limits of Southern Liberalism", *The New Yorker*, Aug. 10, 2009.

Herring, Scott, "After Fifty Years, Atticus Finch Shows Some Wear", *New English Review*, Nov., 2011.

Johnson, Claudia Durst, *Understanding* To Kill a

Mockingbird: *A Student Casebook to Issues, Sources and Historic Documents*. Westport, Conn.: Greenwood Press Literature in Context Series, 1994.

Johnson, Vernon, "A Memoir: Growing up Poor and White in the South" (unpublished memoir, 1993); printed in Claudia Johnson, (q.v.), 157-165.

Lubet, Steven, "Reconstructing Atticus Finch", *Michigan Law Review* vol. 97 (1999), 1339-1362.

Metress, Christopher, "The Rise and Fall of Atticus Finch", *The Chattahoochee Review*, vol. 24 (2003); reprinted in Bloom (q.v.), 141-148.

Pilgrim, David, "The Mammy Caricature", Ferris State University Jim Crow Museum of Racist Memorabilia, http://www.ferris.edu/htmls/news/jimcrow/mammies/

Richards, Gary, "Harper Lee and the Destabilization of Heterosexuality", in Gary Richards, *Lovers and Beloveds: Sexual Otherness in Southern Fiction*, 1936-1961. Baton Rouge: Louisiana State University Press, 2005; reprinted in Bloom (q.v.), 149-188.

Sundquist, Eric J., "Blues for Atticus Finch: Scottsboro, Brown and Harper Lee", in Griffin, Larry J. and Don H. Doyle, eds., *The South as an American Problem*. Athens: University of Georgia Press, 1995; reprinted in Bloom, (q.v.), 75-114.

INDEX

First published in 2012 by
Connell Guides
Spye Arch House
Spye Park
Lacock
Chippenham
Wiltshire SN15 2PR

10 9 8 7 6 5 4 3 2 1

Picture credits:
p.17 © Peter Newark American Pictures/ Bridgeman Art Library
p.25 © Corbis
p.30 © Corbis
p.35 © Silver Screen Collection/ Getty Images
p.57 © Silver Screen Collection/ Getty Images
p.71 © Everett Collection/ Rex Features
p.79 © Corbis

A CIP catalogue record for this book is available from the British Library.
ISBN 978-1-907776-12-0

Design © Nathan Burton
Editorial assistant: Katie Sanderson
Printed in Great Britain by Butler Tanner & Dennis

www.connellguides.com